ARTHUR TAIT

# A Story of Staple Inn on Holborn Hill

*"There was not a quieter spot in England than this.
In all the hundreds of years since London was built, it has not been able
to sweep its roaring tide over that little island of quiet."*

NATHANIEL HAWTHORNE, 1855

INSTITUTE OF ACTUARIES

*For Ann*

Title page illustration:
*Staple Inn court. Watercolour by John Crowther, 1882*
© Guildhall Library, Corporation of London

© Arthur Tait
Published by the Institute of Actuaries 2001
ISBN 0-901066-74-5

# Contents

| | | |
|---|---|---|
| **INTRODUCTION** | | v |
| **ACKNOWLEDGEMENTS** | | vi |
| **1** | **EARLY HISTORY OF THE AREA** | 7 |
| 1.1 | A grassy hill | 7 |
| 1.2 | First inhabitants | 7 |
| 1.3 | The Romans and the birth of London from the first to fourth centuries AD | 7 |
| 1.4 | The Saxons and Lundenwic, from the fifth to eighth centuries AD | 8 |
| 1.5 | Return to London and growth of trade in the ninth and tenth centuries | 8 |
| 1.6 | Tensions between Westminster and City of London, from 1050 onwards | 8 |
| **2** | **WOOL TRADE AT LE STAPLED HALLE FROM THE TWELFTH TO THE FOURTEENTH CENTURIES** | 10 |
| 2.1 | Holborn Bars established, about 1130 | 10 |
| 2.2 | Ely Fair, from the twelfth century | 10 |
| 2.3 | Staples established, from the thirteenth century | 10 |
| 2.4 | The Society of the Merchants of the Staple formed in 1248 | 11 |
| 2.5 | Royal interest in trade at Holborn in the thirteenth century | 11 |
| 2.6 | *Le Stapled Halle* at Holborn, from the late thirteenth century | 12 |
| 2.7 | Fourteenth-century neighbours of *le Stapled Halle* | 12 |
| 2.8 | Growth of trade at *le Stapled Halle* from the 1270s to the 1350s | 13 |
| 2.9 | The road through Holborn and the 'Heavy Hill' | 14 |
| 2.10 | Decline of trade at *le Stapled Halle* from the 1350s to the 1370s | 15 |
| 2.11 | End of trade at *le Stapled Halle*, about 1375 | 16 |
| 2.12 | The Peasants' Revolt of 1381 | 16 |
| **3** | **LAWYERS COME TO HOLBORN IN THE THIRTEENTH AND FOURTEENTH CENTURIES** | 17 |
| 3.1 | Law merchants at Staples | 17 |
| 3.2 | The Woolsack | 17 |
| 3.3 | A royal system of justice emerges in the twelfth and thirteenth centuries | 17 |
| 3.4 | England's 'Third University' emerges in the late thirteenth century | 18 |
| 3.5 | Serjeants' Inns and Inns of Court, in the late eleventh to fourteenth centuries | 19 |
| 3.6 | Inns of Chancery as medieval law schools | 19 |
| **4** | **THE SOCIETY OF STAPLE INN, AND INN OF CHANCERY, 1400–1580** | 20 |
| 4.1 | Birth of the Society of Staple Inn and the Inn of Chancery, 1400–1415 | 20 |
| 4.2 | Staple Inn linked to Gray's Inn | 20 |
| 4.3 | Membership of the Society of Staple Inn | 20 |
| 4.4 | Students at Staple Inn | 20 |
| 4.5 | Society of Staple Inn buildings and setting, 1400–1580 | 21 |
| 4.6 | Middle Row's shadow over Staple Inn, from about 1500 | 22 |
| 4.7 | Outside the parish | 23 |
| 4.8 | The scene towards the City until 1580 | 23 |
| 4.9 | The road to Tyburn, from 1388 | 23 |
| 4.10 | The Society adopts the Woolsack Insignia, about 1553 | 24 |

*Contents continued overleaf*

## CONTENTS

**5 STAPLE INN 1580–1700: FROM PROSPERITY TO DIFFICULTY** 26
5.1 Major rebuilding, 1580–1592 26
5.2 Stained glass in the Hall, 1581–1618 27
5.3 'The Fayrest Inne of Chauncery in this Universitie', 1615 30
5.4 Looking for the Old Bourne: the Magic of the Water 30
5.5 Inhabitants of Staple Inn from the 1550s to 1700 31
5.6 Life at Staple Inn in the late sixteenth and seventeenth centuries 32
5.7 Impact of London's expanding population, 1600–1700 35
5.8 'Cavaliers' or 'Roundheads'? 38
5.9 The Great Plague strikes Staple Inn in 1665 39
5.10 The 1666 Great Fire misses Staple Inn and leaves a 221-year legacy 41
5.11 The Society of Staple Inn in a sorry state in the late seventeenth century 44

**6 RECOVERY AND TRANSITION FROM LAW SCHOOL TO 'CLUB' IN THE EIGHTEENTH CENTURY** 45
6.1 Major rebuilding at Staple Inn, 1729–1780 45
6.2 New stained glass 1747–1880 – but why none during 1618–1747? 47
6.3 Staple Inn becomes 'practically a Club' 49
6.4 Principals of the Society of Staple Inn, 1400–1884 49
6.5 Some eighteenth- and nineteenth-century residents of Staple Inn 50
6.6 Social decline in eighteenth-century Holborn 51
6.7 The Gordon Riots, 1780 55

**7 NINETEENTH-CENTURY STAPLE INN UNTIL 1884 – EVER MORE A 'LITTLE NOOK'** 56
7.1 Condition of London around nineteenth-century Staple Inn 56
7.2 Sanitation in nineteenth-century London 58
7.3 An American view of Staple Inn in 1855: 'that little island of quiet' 60
7.4 Anthony Trollope's observations on 'quiet, dingy nooks' in 1864 60
7.5 Demolition of Middle Row, 1867 60
7.6 Charles Dickens and Staple Inn as 'a little nook', 1853 and 1870 62
7.7 Commuter transport improves in the second half of the 19th century 63
7.8 Thomas Carlyle: London – a place to visit rather than live 64
7.9 The Society of Staple Inn – worth more dead than alive? 65

**8 UNDER NEW MANAGEMENT INTO THE TWENTIETH CENTURY** 67
8.1 Sale of Staple Inn and the end of the Society of Staple Inn, 1884 67
8.2 Public opinion before the auction of Staple Inn, 1886 68
8.3 Auction of Staple Inn, November 1886 69
8.4 The Institute of Actuaries rents Staple Inn Hall, 1887 69
8.5 1887 restoration work 70

**9 TWENTIETH-CENTURY TRIUMPHS OVER ADVERSITY, AND REJUVENATION** 71
9.1 The actuaries and early improvements to the buildings 71
9.2 1914–1936 72
9.3 Rebuilding the Tudor frontage, 1936–1939 74
9.4 The Second World War, and disaster in 1944 75
9.5 Rebuilding and return, 1954–1955 77
9.6 City of London boundaries include Staple Inn, 1994 79
9.7 Refurbishment including Staple Inn Hall, 1993–1998 79
9.8 The actuaries and twentieth-century rejuvenation of Staple Inn 83
9.9 Twentieth-century regeneration around Staple Inn 84

**10 IMAGES OF THE PAST** 85

**11 CONFIDENCE IN THE FUTURE** 87
11.1 Staple Inn and the City 87
11.2 Structural and business continuity in a changing world 87
11.3 Professional continuity in a changing world 87
11.4 Legal continuity over 900 years 87
11.5 Past, present and future 88

**REFERENCES** 89

**INDEX** 91

# Introduction

THE INSTITUTE OF ACTUARIES, which has leased part of Staple Inn including the Hall since May 1887, has the motto '*Certum ex Incertis*' – 'Certainty out of Uncertainty'. Actuaries seek to bring sense to bear on the many doubts we have about how the future will work out. Other professional people based in the Inn, including lawyers, patent agents, accountants, and surveyors, also seek to produce greater certainty for their clients amid the world's many uncertainties.

The historian may perhaps approach the issue of 'certainty' with a broader brush. In addition to huge gaps in knowledge about the past, 'history' is full of different perceptions of the same 'objective' facts. My wife started school in Scotland, and was utterly clear that every battle against the English had been won by the Scots – until she moved to an English school. Knowledge gaps, and differing contexts and perceptions, give the student of history the wonderful opportunity to stretch the imagination and to question what might have been.

- Why has human activity at Staple Inn evolved in the ways it has?
- What impact has the wider London scene had on life at Staple Inn, and what has Staple Inn given back in return?
- Why did the wool trade rise and fall in Holborn?
- What might 'splitting hairs' have to do with student lawyers in Staple Inn?
- Were occupants of Staple Inn Roundheads or Cavaliers, or both, in the Civil War?
- What was it like in Staple Inn during the Great Plague and London's Great Fire?
- What is the history of the early eighteenth-century shoe found concealed in the walls during the 1936 rebuilding?
- Why did some Principals of the Society of Staple Inn donate stained glass panels for the Hall windows, but not others?
- From how far did people come to seek benefit from the alleged medicinal qualities of the water in the courtyard well? Did they ever benefit beyond the admirable quenching of thirst and the occasional aiding of cleanliness?
- Why did the Society of Staple Inn sell up in 1884?
- How much of the Hall roof was salvaged from the flying bomb destruction of 1944 and reused?
- How have the Elizabethan buildings on the road front survived, almost uniquely, for more than four centuries?

This account of the evolution of activity at and near Staple Inn owes much to the 1964 booklet written by actuary Maurice Ogborn[33], and to earlier works by E. Williams[55] and T.C. Worsfold[58]. It seeks to broaden the canvas by suggesting the wider context in which life at Staple Inn developed; to give some clues about what life was like there; and to take advantage of recent research, discovery and writing to bring the story up-to-date.

The selection of material for a book of this length inevitably omits much that is available. There is a wealth of evidence about life in this part of London for the interested to pursue. For simplicity, sources I have cited retain the same reference number in the text and are listed alphabetically by author at the end. For those with little reading time, or with particular interests to follow, the sections into which the book is divided may provide helpful short cuts.

Do not believe everything you read, but let your imagination roam and your own view form as you suppose what might have been. Staple Inn is a lovely place now, with a fine future ahead – and it is wonderfully full of the ghosts of the past. Can you hear them and see them?

# Acknowledgements

I AM GRATEFUL to the Institute of Actuaries for allowing me to write this story and to others in the Inn and elsewhere who have helped me with much advice and information. They are too numerous to list here – actuaries, Institute staff, others working in the Inn, family and friends, but in particular I thank Mervyn Bryn-Jones, Gregor Campbell, Chris Lewin, Robin Michaelson and Peter Tompkins for very helpful steers on the shape and focus of this book; Professor John Baker of St Catharine's College, Cambridge University, for valuable advice on the stained glass; David Raymont for much research and practical assistance; Katrina Malone for proof-reading; and Ian Crane who kindly prepared the index.

My thanks extend to Prudential Corporation plc for access to their archives; the Corporation of London Guildhall Library for viewing of maps and prints reproduced here by kind permission; Holborn and Camden Library Local Studies and Archives Centre; the Victoria & Albert Museum and Northampton Central Art Museum for opinions on the eighteenth-century pewter plates and shoe patten found at Staple Inn in 1938.

The many shortcomings are entirely to be laid at my door. Perhaps readers who spot some of them will pass their comments to the Institute.

**PICTURE SOURCES**

The Prudential Corporation plc has kindly allowed free use of images of Staple Inn Hall, its fine stained glass and archives. Lewis Photos Ltd. photographed the windows. Fine prints serving the story come with permission from the Guildhall Library's impressive Collage database of artworks in its collections.

The Institute of Actuaries has acquired some original interpretations of Staple Inn which are included, whilst various specialist picture libraries, as indicated by each illustration, have been helpful in supply of images of London on the doorstep of Staple Inn in Holborn and beyond.

All efforts have been made to contact copyright holders but if any have been inadvertently overlooked, the Institute of Actuaries will be pleased to make the necessary arrangement at the first opportunity.

*Arthur Tait, August 2001*

# CHAPTER ONE
## *Early History of the Area*

### § 1.1 A GRASSY HILL

As the Ice Age retreated about 10,000 years ago and England, Scotland and Wales became an island, separate from the rest of Europe, three hills stood close together above the northern marshy edges of the River Thames. Two were flat-topped gravel hills, with a stream between them. The third was a grassy hill across a river. The first two, Cornhill and Ludgate Hill, with the stream Walbrook between them, became the site of the City of London. The third hill, across the river Fleet, became High Holborn, home of Staple Inn.

The grassy hill was fertile, with many springs and streams. However it was further from the Thames than the other two hills, and a less obvious site for human settlement. It stood halfway between the lowest fordable point across the river, at Westminster, and the place downstream where the gravel enabled a bridge to be built across the Thames on reasonable foundations.

Geography thus decreed that the Staple Inn area would be unlikely to become a dominating centre of human activity, but enabled it to foster a strong supporting role. As the years went by it provided a major road into and out of the City of London, extensive agriculture and gardening, centres for customs and trade, for religion, law, hospitals and cemeteries, and for expert professional, educational and commercial services. The grassy hill became the site for important links between the City and Westminster, between the City and the rest of England and between the City and countries overseas.

### § 1.2 FIRST INHABITANTS

The first known people in the Greater London area were hunters from 10,000 BC or earlier. There are signs of them in Westminster, and it would be surprising if they had not hunted over the grassy hill, so near the river.

The first known road in the area was built by the Romans when they arrived in 43 AD or in the next very few years. It went from Colchester to Silchester, south-east of Reading, via Holborn, by-passing the two gravel hills, which at that time were of no significance. From their earliest days in Britain the Romans brought human activity to the area now occupied by Staple Inn.

### § 1.3 THE ROMANS AND THE BIRTH OF LONDON FROM THE FIRST TO FOURTH CENTURIES

The first known settlers near Holborn were the Romans. They began to build a trading centre on the two gravel hills and down to the Thames by 50 AD. They developed more road systems, including the Pretorian Way. From Richborough in Kent this crossed the Thames by the gravel hills, left London at Newgate, came across the deep Fleet river valley and up the considerable hill to High Holborn, along Oxford Street and on to Wroxeter in Shropshire – the routes of today's A2 and A5 roads.

The upper reaches of the Holborn hill were a good staging post for travellers. Nearer the City the steep valley through which the 'bourne in the hole' or 'stream in the valley' flowed was unsuitable. After a gentle start at Hampstead the stream passed through almost ravine-like slopes to the Holborn bridge to join the tidal inlet of the Fleet river.

Holborn can reasonably claim to be the first suburb of London.

People living at this staging post saw the ebb and flow of Roman occupation over nearly 400 years. They saw and felt the force of Queen Boadicea plundering Roman London in 60 AD when the legions were far away in the north-west, leaving behind half metre thick fire debris. They saw London's population grow to at least 50,000 by 100 AD. They saw a huge fort cover 15 acres, the base for 15,000 soldiers and the administrative centre for Roman Britain, where the Museum of London now stands. They witnessed 100 acres destroyed by fire in 115 AD.

They saw, and perhaps contributed to, a great wall built about 200 AD, near to but not enclosing them, passing 180 metres to the east of the Fleet river. The wall went two miles round the City, used 85,000 tons of Kentish ragstone, brought 70 miles by boat, to a height of up to six metres, with a two metre deep defensive ditch outside it. The building of Newgate in the wall reinforced the importance of the Pretorian Way in the Roman scheme of things. Excavations near Holborn Viaduct Station suggested that there might have been an amphitheatre outside Newgate, where the Fleet's steep ravine provided a natural site similar to many other Roman theatres. The discovery of an amphitheatre under the Guildhall in 1988, however, casts some doubt on this.

Later they saw London's population decline from more than 50,000 to no more than 30,000 by the year 400.

### § 1.4 THE SAXONS AND LUNDENWIC, FROM THE FIFTH TO EIGHTH CENTURIES AD

By 410 the Romans had left London, withdrawing across the Channel to deal with problems at home as the Visigoths successfully besieged Rome. London was largely deserted and fell into decay.

In the sixth century Anglo-Saxons came from Denmark, northern Germany and Jutland to fill the vacuum. From about 600, if not before, they felt sufficiently secure to follow their natural style and develop a town with a port outside the Roman walls. Known as *Lundenwic* this stretched along a gravel bank above the marshes from near the Fleet to the north end of today's Trafalgar Square and Drury Lane, with settlements further on towards Westminster at the marshy Isle of Thanet.

Trade expanded, with textile, metal and bone industries, and cloth weaving the main export. *Lundenwic* developed a money economy, with taxation, and became a major Christian city by the eighth century, with a population of about 10,000. There were well-maintained streets, arranged in a grid system. A five-metre wide north–south street was resurfaced at least ten times in 200 years. Excavations at the Royal Opera House in 1998 found the northern boundary of *Lundenwic* there to have been a deep fortified ditch. It had extended to within a few hundred metres of the future site of Staple Inn, to beyond the modern Kingsway and Fleet Street.

Since the road through Holborn was busy, it is a reasonable guess that the grassy hill was the scene of much activity. The Thames was barely half a mile away, several hundred metres wider than today. The area offered arable fields, pastures, meadows, brooks and watermills as well as the road.

### § 1.5 RETURN TO LONDON AND GROWTH OF TRADE IN THE NINTH AND TENTH CENTURIES

From 842 the Danes frequently invaded the area, and local people began to move back inside the old Roman walls for security. By 886 Alfred the Great occupied London, converting the small riverside village to a port and market town again. *Lundenwic* was largely deserted for the next two hundred years, its timber buildings falling into decay.

As *Lundenwic* declined London's commerce expanded. The Saxon Kings held markets all over England. Holborn's place on the key trade route between the west and London's port became more important. Its population grew. A timber-built St. Andrew's Church existed by 951 on the site of the present church near Holborn Bridge, one of the earliest churches in the London area. By the year 1000 there were only three or four churches in London and two or three in the remains of *Lundenwic*.

By the tenth century trade became so significant that a royal ordinance sought to regulate it and fix tolls in London, covering such goods as wine, fish, planks of wood and farm produce, and possibly also wool and cloth.

### § 1.6 TENSIONS BETWEEN WESTMINSTER AND CITY OF LONDON, FROM 1050 ONWARDS

Canute, King of England from 1016 to 1035, although much misunderstood in folklore when he tried to show his courtiers that only God could control the tide, was much more successful providing firm government, security against external

Viking threats, and uniting Danes and Saxons. By 1050 Edward the Confessor started to establish Westminster as the royal centre of government, and a clear division between it and the trading focus of the City began to emerge.

In 1066, after victory at Hastings, William the Conqueror needed the political and economic support of London. Unsure about success with direct attack, he devastated the land to the north and west (including Holborn?), until London acknowledged him and invited him to coronation at Westminster on Christmas Day 1066. Despite his wish that his claim to the throne should be seen as lawful and peaceful, his followers, fearing opposition, pillaged the houses in the area. Subsequently William's *Domesday* survey reported that he had two cottagers in the Holborn hamlet.

During the following centuries a strong king could dominate London, but when the king was weak London's ruling élite were able to win royal agreement to greater freedom to manage their own affairs. In about 1135 Stephen recognised London as a commune, a self-governing urban confederation with the right to choose its own officials and collect its own taxes. This was diluted later in the century, but hostility against high taxation to pay for the Crusades of the absent Richard I, and his own weakness, caused King John to sign the *Magna Carta* at Runnymede in 1215. He granted London a new charter, including the right to an annually elected mayor. London's constitution, with a mayor elected by the citizens of the City and 24 (25 after 1394) aldermen, remained through the Middle Ages, and is recognisable today.

Freedom from arbitrary royal taxation, however, was not part of the 1215 deal, a key point for the future development of Staple Inn.

CHAPTER TWO

# *Wool Trade at le Stapled Halle from the Twelfth to the Fourteenth Centuries*

§ 2.1 HOLBORN BARS ESTABLISHED, ABOUT 1130

During the twelfth century, as more houses were built on the main roads out of London, the City's outer limits were marked with stones some distance outside the walls. Later these were replaced by chains, and then by bars to control access by traders and by undesirable characters such as vagabonds and lepers.

The road outside the future site of Staple Inn was chosen as one such control point since the steep slopes on either side of the Fleet made the ground nearer the City unsuitable. The Holborn Bars were set up in about 1130 at the place marked today by the granite obelisks surmounted by silver dragons immediately outside Staple Inn. The eighteenth-century Bars appear in *The Four Stages of Cruelty* of 1751 by William Hogarth (1697–1764).

Packhorse trains and merchants stopped at the Bars for rest and business. This road was the main route for the transport of wool and other goods from the Cotswolds and further west to London's port, and for the return of imports bought in exchange. The volume of activity grew as wool and weaving became major business between England and continental Europe.

§ 2.2 ELY FAIR, FROM THE TWELFTH CENTURY

Across the road to the north there was, possibly from Saxon times, a fair among the gardens, orchards, farms, streams, and watermills of Holborn. This Portepool Fair, covering 40 acres, became known as Ely Fair after the Bishop of Ely acquired the area late in the twelfth century. The name is preserved in Ely Place. Traces of a pool were found under the eastern part of the building constructed near there by the Prudential Assurance Company nearly one thousand years later. The Fair became an important centre for international trade.

As London expanded with the growth of foreign trade and migration from other parts of Britain and from overseas, its international character was reinforced – and has never since been lost. A study of London's children at the end of the twentieth century identified at least 307 languages, with hundreds more dialects[2]. The area around Holborn Bars and Ely Fair eight centuries earlier did not match that scale of linguistic diversity, but it set a pattern that was never broken. The Fair attracted people from many countries, including Holland, Flanders, France, Germany, Italy, Scandinavia, Spain and further east, and reinforced the strategic position of Holborn Bars on the Holborn road as an important place for international business.

Fairs, with annual regulation and often with international dimensions, contrasted with markets, under weekly regulation and satisfying day-to-day needs. The market at Ely Place became famous for its produce, including roses and strawberries mentioned in Shakespeare's *Richard III* when Richard was Protector planning young Edward V's coronation – 'My Lord Bishop of Ely, you have very good strawberries at your garden in Holborn, I require you let us have a mess of those'. In 1372 the Bishop's gardener sold onions, garlic, turnips, leeks, parsley, herbs and beans on the pod.

§ 2.3 STAPLES ESTABLISHED, FROM THE THIRTEENTH CENTURY

Centres for business were established near the Bars at each main trade route into London. These trading centres were often referred to as Staple Halls, or 'Staples' – or *le Stapled Halle*, as in Holborn, and as recorded in 1330 and 1333 outside the City gates at Bishopsgate and near the Tower.

The word 'staple' has had many meanings, including a heap (of goods); a rest, support or stand on which goods could be stored off the ground; a post, pillar or stone to mark the boundary or location of a store; a storehouse; a market house;

a warehouse for examining and taxing goods liable to export duties; a customs-house, especially for wool; and more recently a basic commodity as in 'staple diet', or a U-shaped piece of metal or wire. It was probably applied to the Holborn *Stapled Halle* to describe an aisled timber-built hall, providing a covered market with pillars as well as open space outside, before it became a customs-house. (In modern French *halle* still means a covered market.)

Later, 'Staple' towns were lucrative distribution and tax centres through which the king required exports to pass, closely linked with the Exchequer (named after the chequer-board table-cloth on which accounts were originally settled) and the Chancery (to which offences and disputes were referred).

§ 2.4 THE SOCIETY OF THE MERCHANTS OF THE STAPLE FORMED IN 1248

The Society of the Merchants of the Staple was formed in 1248 and incorporated in 1319, with wool its main object of trade. This was England's first great trading company. Mayors of the Staple were appointed to certify the sale of woolsacks and to levy tax. Merchants travelled widely to find and buy wool, arrange for it to be packed, sealed and transported, seek sales, and to extract and exchange the sale price into English coins from many foreign currencies, often months after the sale since credit was regularly given; and to seek resolution of disputes.

Involved with Staples in many locations, the Society had no special links with *le Stapled Halle* in Holborn. Its legal base was initially in Westminster, and it never made Holborn its headquarters. Although the Westminster Staple was moved to Holborn in 1375 for a short period as part of political infighting at the end of Edward II's reign, it was sent back to Westminster a few years later, and on to Leadenhall in 1463.

§ 2.5 ROYAL INTEREST IN TRADE AT HOLBORN IN THE THIRTEENTH CENTURY

Late in the twelfth century Richard I gave the collection of custom at Holborn Bars to the Bishop of Ely. The attractions of this site were so obvious that the City of London tried to take possession in about 1220, annexing Holborn road up to the Bars, but failing to acquire the land to the north and of the future *le Stapled Halle* to the south.

In the thirteenth century London continued to enjoy or endure varying pressures from the Crown, normally related to royal needs for money to finance wars and for political support. These demands were sometimes acceptable to the citizens in the interests of trade stability. At other times exorbitant demands for money or the grant of key trading rights to foreigners were strongly resented. The political leverage available to the king through the granting of wool-trading rights to different groups and places caused the volumes of trade passing through Holborn to rise and fall.

Henry III tried to transfer much of the Holborn business to Westminster, establishing a fair there in competition with Ely Fair. The Bishop of Ely and the merchants blocked him. But the saga had hardly begun.

In 1253 Henry III obtained stronger control of the wool trade at Holborn Bars for his relatives, through the well-worn device of the marriage of a young boy to a young girl. Robert, the Earl of Derby, who was made a ward of the King at age nine when his father died, had inherited control of the wool court at Holborn. His seven-year old bride, Mary le Brun, was the King's half-brother's daughter.

In 1256 the King confirmed a charter enabling approved merchants to access Chancery Lane, and thence the new Temple and the Thames, from outside the Bars, subject only to paying the King's tax. The official tax collector, the 'middle man' Bishop, was by-passed – an early example of tax avoidance. The King's control was strengthened when his son acquired these rights for the Duchy of Lancaster in 1266. This ploy backfired, however, as Chancery Lane could not cope with the traffic, and before the end of the century it was closed to carts and carriages as unsafe. Perhaps anticipating this, Edward I 'completed the circle' in 1286 by appointing his detested tax-gathering chancellor as Bishop of Ely. Ely Palace and St Etheldreda's Church were built soon after.

In addition to taxes, for much of the thirteenth century the kings looked to resident Jews for substantial extra funds. Jews were allowed by their religion to lend money for profit, which Christians were not. However, the Jews' ability to pay was strained by growing royal demands, partly due to Edward I being at war simultaneously with the French, Scots and Welsh. Various actions were taken to encourage a sufficient flow of Jewish money to the King. The House of Converts and Rolls Chapel were built in Chancery Lane immediately south of the future *le Stapled Halle* in 1228–1232 for Jews willing to convert to Christianity. Other incentives were created for Jewish money to line the royal purse – but they failed. In 1290 Jews were officially expelled from England, and other sources of income were needed.

More tax on wool, England's largest trading commodity, provided an answer. It also caused the development of *le Stapled Halle* in its particular form in Holborn.

### § 2.6 LE STAPLED HALLE AT HOLBORN, FROM THE LATE THIRTEENTH CENTURY

In 1180 the present Staple Inn area was in two separate parts covering the east and west of today's site. The Dean and Chapter of St Paul's purchased the east part in 1183 for 2 marks (and 2d to the vendor's wife). It was an open plot with about 30 feet frontage to Holborn road and 597 feet depth, taking it to the boundary with the Bishop of Chichester's garden down the hill towards Fleet Street. The properties passed through various hands in the next hundred years. In 1308 the depth from the road reduced to 225 feet, close to the present southern boundary.

When the Bars were first established traders camped outside in the wide roadway, perhaps with a small street market. Any buildings would have been small. As trade expanded after 1270 (see section 2.8) that area became inadequate for the business, lodgings, stabling and storage needs. There was no space available to the north of the road, occupied by the Bishop of Ely. There was space on the open land to the south, on the present Staple Inn site. A trading centre was established there.

The first record of buildings at Staple Inn is in 1292[33], and they were probably there some years earlier. (The first Customs House in the City was built in 1275.)

There were two separate buildings with one owner. One was on the site of the present Hall. The other was similarly set back from the road, in the south-east corner of today's courtyard, where No. 9 now stands. This was *le Stapled Halle*.

Early owners of *le Stapled Halle* included a cobbler and a chancery clerk, the latter probably involved with the wool trade. That connection was clear in 1328 when ownership was with Richard Starcolf, citizen and mercer, and in 1340 with a Constable of the Staple.

Very little is known about these early buildings. In his 1598 *Survey of London* John Stow confessed ignorance about the origins of Staple Inn and about the buildings which preceded the structures put up in the 1580s[46]. The only part of that Hall remaining now may be parts of the glass in the two lower middle panels of windows on the south side of the present Hall and the window for Nicholas Brocket on the north. (See section 5.2.)

Tenements at *le Stapled Halle* were leased to people for the conduct of business and for merchants' accommodation. Goods were weighed, taxed, stored and sold, and lodgings and stabling provided. Traders were sometimes required to stay at least fifteen days at the Staple to help to ensure the business was done properly. The goods included wool, cloth, leather, and wine, with wool pre-eminent. Today's courtyard was then a large open space between the road and the buildings.

### § 2.7 FOURTEENTH-CENTURY NEIGHBOURS OF LE STAPLED HALLE

There were fewer than 200 houses in Holborn in 1332, although some were large. Intersecting paths crossed meadows between Holborn road, Shoe Lane, Fleet Street and Chancery Lane.

On the east boundary of *le Stapled Halle* was a large garden and property owned by a King's Justice, and from 1370 by the Monastery of Malmesbury. (After the Dissolution of the Monasteries in 1539 it passed to a John Beaumont, and later after various name changes was redeveloped around Furnival Street.)

On the west side of *le Stapled Halle* were the Norman buildings and ruins of

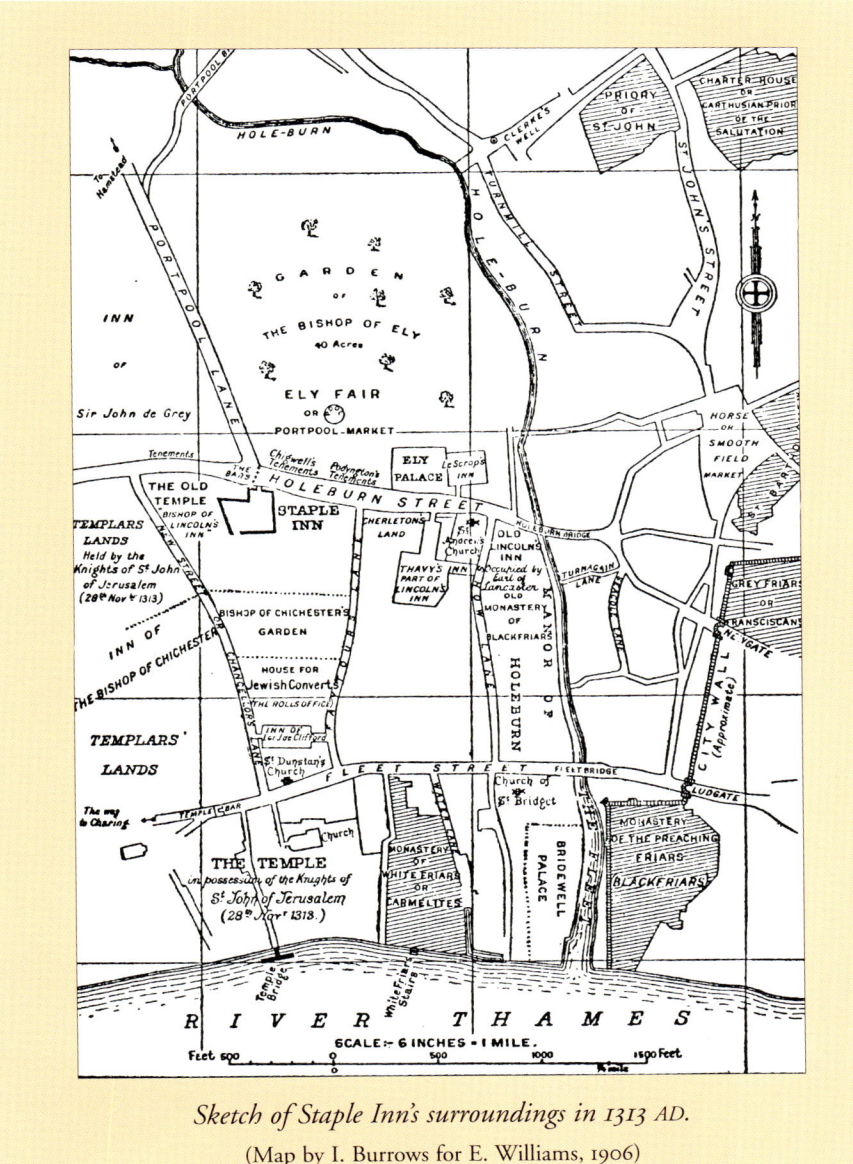

*Sketch of Staple Inn's surroundings in 1313 AD.*
(Map by I. Burrows for E. Williams, 1906)

the round church that the Knights Templar had built in 1128 and sold to the Bishop of Lincoln in 1186. (Ownership passed to the Earl of Southampton in 1540, and Southampton Buildings now occupy the site.)

To the south of *le Stapled Halle* were the extensive gardens of the Bishop of Chichester and of the House of Converts (see section 2.5). In 1377 the latter was assigned to the Keeper of the Rolls of Chancery. (Until recently part of the Public Record Office was on this site.)

On three sides *le Stapled Halle* was surrounded by substantial peace and quiet. On the fourth side trade by the Bars produced sharply contrasting bustle and turmoil.

## § 2.8 GROWTH OF TRADE AT LE STAPLED HALLE FROM THE 1270S TO THE 1350S

For many years until 1270 most English wool was exported to the continent. The trade was largely under Flemish control, conducted through various provincial centres such as Boston, Hull, Lynn and Southampton. London's share was small.

This changed dramatically in 1270 when a political dispute led to the arrest of Flemish merchants. Their place as importers of goods for exchange with wool was taken mainly by Italian and Hanseatic (North German) merchants.

The latter chose to delegate to London merchants much of the wool purchase in the provincial fairs for export, increasingly through London, in return for wax, sugar, almonds, alum, spices and luxury cloth imports. This gave them a good price for the wool. It also enabled safe convoy systems to shepherd their ships from London to the continent during the frequent naval wars and amid perpetual danger from pirates.

In 1275 Edward I's need for money led him to rationalise the ad hoc taxation arrangements and to introduce the first regular customs duties on exports of wool, wool felts and leather. The highest tax was on wool. Referring to the popular black-faced sheep, the nursery rhyme 'Baa baa black sheep, have you any wool?' laments the high, two-thirds, taxation burden. 'Yes, sir, yes, sir, three bags full' sounds promising, but the income had to be divided between 'one for my master' – the king, 'one for my dame' – the noble tax collector, and only 'one for the little boy who lives down the lane'.

The tax was levied initially at the various places where exports took place, including London, and was paid by foreign buyers. Later Edward decreed that it should be collected in specified towns (Staples) near the point of use in the Low Countries, and towns such as Dordrecht, Brabant, Malines and Antwerp were chosen. In 1313 Edward II centralised the tax collection to one compulsory Staple at St Omer, and in following years other continental centres were selected.

The new arrangements from 1270 favoured the London merchants against their competitors elsewhere in England, and benefited *le Stapled Halle*'s trade. London's share of England's growing wool exports rose from 25% in the 1280s to 33% in 1297, 40% in the early 1300s and 44% in 1335[56]. 7,000 woolsacks were exported through London every year in the 1280s, 20,000 every year in the 1350s[29].

§ 2.9 THE ROAD THROUGH HOLBORN AND THE 'HEAVY HILL'

Access from *le Stapled Halle* to the trading ships on the Thames was available through Newgate to the City, or by the shorter route a few hundred metres down the hill via the Fleet river. The first mention of inward cargoes on the Fleet up to Holborn Bridge is in the early twelfth century, when stones were brought for the construction of the first St Paul's church. Coal was brought in there from the early thirteenth century.

The road through Holborn became busier, the only good route from the west. The country lane to the south, Fleet Street, was less suitable for heavy traffic. The connecting lane, Chancery Lane, was in bad condition. For at least ten years at the end of the thirteenth century it was barred to carts and carriages as unsafe. (See section 2.5.)

As a main highway much of the Holborn road was wide enough for sixteen armed knights to ride abreast – good space for loaded carts to pass each other. However it brought problems, since no one accepted responsibility for its maintenance. As with other Roman roads its condition deteriorated for many centuries after their departure. The hard Roman surface was buried far beneath the mud and debris of traffic, animals, and neighbouring homes. Carts and wagons created deep ruts.

The road was not paved again until 1417. Then Thomas Rymer (1643?–1713) reports:

> [it] was so deep and miry that many perils and hazards were thereby occasioned as well to the King's carriages passing that way as to those of his subjects[58].

Royal action (under Henry V) ensured fresh paving, with 40 tons of stone. That was not renewed until 1541, when Henry VIII ordered certain streets to be paved with stone since they were 'very foul and full of pits and sloughs, very perilous and noyous as well for the King's subjects on horseback as on foot and with

*St Andrew's Church, Holborn, 1760, with a glimpse of the 'Heavy Hill'.*
From an old print shown by T. Cato Worsfold, 1903. (© Henry Bumpus, publisher)

carriages.' Chancery Lane and the Holborn road were among those chosen for repaving.

A particular feature of the Holborn road was the hill up from Holborn Bridge over the Fleet. Steeper than the hill from the City side to the bridge, this 'Heavy Hill' had an average gradient on its incline up to St Andrew's Church of at least 1 in 8, and was probably as steep as 1 in 7 in places. It well deserved its name for the difficulty it caused travellers, whether or not, later, they were prisoners on their way from Newgate or Fleet prisons to the gallows at Tyburn (Marble Arch). Especially in the winter it must have tested the nerves, patience and stamina of many a mud-spattered traveller, horse and wagon-driver. How many loads of wool, hides, cheese, corn, wine, coal and wood tumbled out of control down that hill? Were the less scrupulous at hand to 'help' with recovery?

## § 2.10 DECLINE OF TRADE AT LE STAPLED HALLE FROM THE 1350S TO THE 1370S

After 75 years' growing prosperity from the 1270s, the scene changed sharply for the worse for *le Stapled Halle* during the second half of the fourteenth century.

There were three main reasons for the decline of trade there. One was the Black Death, the second was the King's money-raising policy, and the third was the increasing retention of English wool for cloth manufacture at home.

Paradoxically, the English capture of Calais in 1347 contributed to the Black Death by reopening the wool trade from there. The plague was transmitted through flea-bites. Rats infested with fleas were the main carriers, but wool and cloth also became infested. A ship from France brought infested cloth to Weymouth in Dorset in July 1348. (Poxwell village is a few miles from Weymouth.) The plague spread rapidly along England's trade routes, and massively to London. Between November 1348 and winter 1350 at least one third of London's 80,000 population died – some estimates quote one half. It was a worse disaster even than the better documented Great Plague of 1665.

The dreadful slaughter impacted badly on confidence and prosperity in London. There were no safer areas in the country to which to flee. The wool trade suffered hugely, as did *le Stapled Halle* through which infested wool was passing.

The plague in London was checked by a severe winter in 1350, but returned in 1361–1362, in 1379, and regularly for nearly three hundred years. London's population was only 50,000 in 1380.

More permanently significant for *le Stapled Halle* was Edward III's money-raising policy. Wage and price inflation following the 1348–1350 decimation of population led the King's Parliament to allow foreign and provincial merchants to compete freely in the City. In 1363 the home staple policy was abandoned in favour of Calais. With short intervals it remained there until the French recaptured it in 1558.

Worse still, after 1363 the King started to sell rights of exemption from taxation to Italians who were allowed to bypass Calais and trade directly with Italy. The Genoese made Southampton their European headquarters in 1388, bypassing London. The King had urgent need of Italian money and Genoese naval support. Wool exports through London fell sharply, to the detriment of local wool merchants.

The third, enduring reason for the decline of trade at *le Stapled Halle* was the increasing retention of English wool at home for local cloth-making from the second half of the fourteenth century. Instead of providing the raw material for continental cloth-makers, England's wool became the foundation for England's own cloth-making industry. Edward III imported Flemish weavers to teach the English the finer arts of weaving. Woollen cloth soon supplanted raw wool as England's major source of wealth-creation and became the country's main export for several centuries. The Flemish cloth industry declined. The Merchants of the Staple also declined, and the Merchant Adventurers rose to pre-eminence in London's business community.

England's annual wool exports fell from 30,000 sacks in early fourteenth century to 19,359 in 1392–1395, 13,625 in 1410–1415, and 7,654 in 1446–1448[30]. Cloth exports rose from 5,000 sacks in 1350 to 40,000 in 1400 and 160,000 by 1490[29].

## CHAPTER TWO

### § 2.11 END OF TRADE AT LE STAPLED HALLE, ABOUT 1375

It is not known exactly when trading at *le Stapled Halle* ended. The clues given here suggest that by about 1370 major decline had set in, and that active trading ceased soon afterwards. T.C. Worsfold states that Staple Inn became an Inn of Chancery in 1378[58]. Other circumstantial evidence broadly supports this, suggesting that lawyers were settling in no later than 1400.

Was there a closing ceremony for the last traders? Did the last man slip quietly away, perhaps even without realising he was the last? Did the incoming lawyers inherit a stock of discarded wool and other goods? Did the pie-powder court law merchants (see section 3.1) simply stay on and start to pick up new legal work? Or was there a short period when the place was empty? Perhaps any such period, if there was one at all, was very short as the owner sought tenants and new legal people applied.

### § 2.12 THE PEASANTS' REVOLT OF 1381

The home manufacture of cloth damaged *le Stapled Halle*, but did provide clothing and work. It also expanded the English language with such gems as 'spin a yarn', 'thread of discourse', 'homespun', 'tenterhooks', 'web of life', 'unravel a mystery', and 'spinster'. More significantly the growth of skilled village manufactures marked a shift from the medieval to more modern society. The 'peasants' began to struggle for more freedom and economic security against the old order of Church and State.

By the 1370s the ageing Edward III's authority was waning. A combination of plague, taxation, war, trade dislocation and hatred of Italians led to civil disorder in London. In 1381 the Peasants' Revolt under Wat Tyler against the poll tax, (the contemporary form of reaction to such a tax), plundered Temple Church, broke open Fleet and Newgate prisons, marched down Fleet Street and destroyed Savoy Palace*, (to mention a few places near *le Stapled Halle*). Many leading people were murdered, notably lawyers, Flemish merchants, and men linked to tax collection and law enforcement. English merchants were spared, which may explain why *le Stapled Halle* survived even though one of the marauding bands 'set afire houses of various people and took away prisoners condemned by the law and returned from Westminster to London by way of Holborn'[43].

Wat Tyler was killed at Smithfield, a few hundred metres from *le Stapled Halle*, and the revolt fizzled out in a few days. The City sought to re-establish its trading rights. Some were restored, but not the trading privileges of the leading wool exporters to the Staple, who were severely damaged. London became very poor.

The road through Holborn, which had deteriorated badly through the prolonged weight of trade and the nil-maintenance highway regime, had a short breather.

---

*After his Savoy Palace was destroyed by the mob in 1381, John of Gaunt lived in Ely Place when not on his frequent travels. In *Richard II* (Act 2, Scene 1) Shakespeare has John at Ely Palace in his embittered, final hours of 1399 speaking up for England but finding it diminished to the status of 'pelting farm' in the wool trade:

This royal throne of kings, this sceptred isle
This earth of majesty, this seat of Mars
This happy breed of men, this little world;
This precious stone set in the silver sea
This blessed plot, this earth, this realm, this England
[…]
This land of such dear souls, this dear dear land,
Dear for her reputation through the world,
Is now leased out, (I die pronouncing it.)
Like to a tenement, or *pelting farm*:
Ah, would the scandal vanish with my life,
How happy then were my ensuing death!

# CHAPTER THREE
## *Lawyers come to Holborn in the Thirteenth and Fourteenth Centuries*

Although the customs-house operation of the Holborn *Stapled Halle* was brief, its location and trading origins gave it a wider significance and the opportunity to evolve a new role when its wool trade vanished.

### § 3.1 LAW MERCHANTS AT STAPLES

Commercial activity and taxation in the Staples inevitably gave rise to disputes. Not everyone engaged in the wool trade was passionately committed to ethical behaviour. Wool was a goldmine for the successful trader and, to mix metaphors, many bees swarmed around that honey-pot. The poet John Gower (ca. 1330–1408) wrote:

> O wool, noble dame, thou art the goddess of merchants, to serve thee they are all ready; by thy good fortune and thy wealth thou makest some mount high, and others bringest to ruin. The staple where thou dwellest is never free of fraud and trickery … In England art thou born, but it is said that thou art but ill governed, for Trick, who hath much money, is made regent of thy staple … so they compass much trickery and many schemes how they may gather thee …[21]

'Trickery', or just straightforward differences of opinion, could involve varying grades, ages and qualities of wool; inclusion of hair, earth, rubbish and moisture in the packed product for weighing; switching of labels; collection of money, the exchange rates used, the use of false coins; 'losses' due to piracy, robbery, storm and fire.

Law merchants were authorised to determine these disputes. Courts of justice held indoors were 'hustings', but the Staples were outdoor 'pie-powder' courts, from the French *pieds poudreux*, where feet were dirty and dusty from travel. The practice of law at *le Stapled Halle* was a necessary adjunct to its trading activity.

Furthermore, the Chancery (Lord Chancellor's) Court was often held in Holborn, rather than in the Westminster Great Hall. It seems probable that before the Inns of Court were established the Chancellor's business was sometimes carried out in the pie-powder court at *le Stapled Halle*.

### § 3.2 THE WOOLSACK

We may speculate that the hard benches provided for visiting legal dignitaries at *le Stapled Halle*, and the length of the sessions they had to endure, caused those with more sensitive posteriors to take advantage of the many woolsacks in the area. By the early fourteenth century the King endorsed this practice, authorising and requiring the Chancellor and judges to sit on woolsacks when performing their legal duties.

The symbol of the source of England's wealth became also a symbol of the Crown's law officers.

### § 3.3 A ROYAL SYSTEM OF JUSTICE EMERGES IN THE TWELFTH AND THIRTEENTH CENTURIES

In the eleventh century legal processes began to develop to help to keep peace in the land, although foreign invasions and royal disputes still provided many interruptions. As the kings began to recognise the need to work through parliaments they convened them for short periods around the country. By the 1170s and 1180s parliaments were more often called to Westminster Hall. From 1248 Henry III confirmed Westminster as the headquarters of a new system of royal justice, strengthening the evolution of common law begun under Henry II.

Westminster Hall remained the royal justice headquarters until 1882 when the Law Courts opened in the Strand.

As the new arrangements developed the kings sought to ensure effective control by insisting that their officers, household servants and chancery clerks should not live in the City unless they were citizens in their own right. Royal and religious palaces and other great mansions along the Strand and Fleet Street became centres for officials and dignitaries associated with the new justice system. The big Inns and houses in the Holborn area became natural homes for many of these people.

### § 3.4 ENGLAND'S 'THIRD UNIVERSITY' EMERGES IN THE LATE THIRTEENTH CENTURY

Until 1207 the role of advocate in courts of law was normally carried out by clergy. The Church was hugely significant, owning perhaps one-third of the nation's property and land. Twenty to twenty-five per cent of London's population, and therefore a high proportion of the better-educated people, were in religious orders. However in 1207 the Church decreed that priests should no longer appear in civil courts as pleaders. It wanted to depress the growing importance of common and merchant law. It failed.

The withdrawal of the clergy and growth of the new royal justice system generated a need for people to be trained in common law. The early academic life of England's two universities, Cambridge and Oxford, was based on the culture and learning of ancient Rome. In the legal field they were concerned only with Roman law. They offered no training in the emerging common law of England, which derived from Anglo-Saxon tribal custom.

Edward I decreed in 1290 and 1292 that law students should be recruited and teaching provided near the Courts in the open countryside between Westminster and the City. This suited the royal concern not to enhance the power of the City. Henry III had decreed as early as 1234 that schools of law and Inns of Apprentices of the law should not be allowed inside the City's walls.

The Lord Chancellor's Department settled in Chancery Lane. From the late thirteenth century chancery clerks moved to rented houses there, from the palaces in which they had been based. Before long a new race of lawyers lived in great houses nearby owned by King's Justices. These became the four Inns of Court. They in turn attracted satellite bodies which became the nine or ten (or at times more) Inns of Chancery. Above them all in the legal hierarchy was the Serjeant's Inn, for judges, of which for a period there were two. The lawyers spread along Chancery Lane from the Temple through Lincoln's Inn to Gray's Inn.

This great centre of legal learning and practice came to be known informally as the Third University of England. The lawyers became the first substantial group of learned laymen in the land. This was significant for England's development, since the 'third university' laid the foundation for a power that could mediate between Crown and people, and in conjunction with Parliament would check and in 1641–1649 stop royal despotism.

It also promoted the nation's distinctive language which Alfred had started to nurture but which had been held in check for three centuries through the use of French by the country's leaders, with their Norman background. Henry II, for instance, King from 1154–1189, spoke almost no English, and Richard I ('*Coeur de Lion*'), King from 1189–1199, never spoke any. The growth of the common law stopped that. In 1362, under Edward III, a parliamentary statute declared that since French was 'much unknown in this Realm' all law court pleadings and judgements were to be spoken in English (although still enrolled in Latin). '*Men of lawr fro that tyme shold plede in her moder tunge*'[52].

The 'mother tongue', which the peasants had kept alive despite their French-speaking masters, received official approval through the lawyers, and became the tongue of the educated and upper class. '*The yere of oure Lorde a thousand thre hundred and foure score and fyve in alle the gramere scoles of Engelond, children leveth Frensche and construeth and lerneth in Englische.*'

The chronicler also noted a '*disavauntage*', that there '*is harme for them if they schulle passe the see and travaille in strange landes and in many other places*'. English aversion to foreign languages has early origins.

The English language developed through writers such as Geoffrey Chaucer (whose *Canterbury Tales* were written circa 1387) and John Wycliffe, and in legal Holborn, especially from 1476 through Caxton's printing press down the road in Westminster.

The grassy hill was finding a powerful new role.

## § 3.5 SERJEANTS' INNS AND INNS OF COURT, IN THE LATE ELEVENTH TO FOURTEENTH CENTURIES

The first lawyers' Inn was established in the late eleventh century at Scrope's Inn opposite St Andrew's Church near Holborn Bridge. It was a Serjeants' Inn, for judges, superior in status to Inns of Court. In 1498 it moved to the Temple.

The original Lincoln's Inn was also near St. Andrew's Church, at the north end of Shoe Lane, on the site of the Black Friars monastery. From about 1286 the Earl of Lincoln provided residence there for clerks and law students who helped his business. He had wonderful gardens and orchards, but their attractions were compromised by the growing stench from the river Fleet nearby. No longer could ten to twelve ships berth near Holborn Bridge, as the waste from tanneries, other industry and people accumulated in the river down towards the Thames. In 1290 the White Friars petitioned Parliament that the putrid exhalations from the Fleet overcame the aroma of their incense and had brought the lives of several brothers to an untimely end.

Through marriage, (often the most convenient way to acquire property otherwise not available), the Earl of Lincoln in 1313 added much of the west side of Chancery Lane to the land on the east side, immediately west of Staple Inn, which he had acquired from the Knights Templar in 1186. By 1330–1335 he had moved his operations from the stinking Fleet to the agreeable area where Lincoln's Inn now stands.

North of Holborn Bars, Sir Reginald Gray, Chief Justice of Chester, acquired in 1294 the Manor House of the 'Ancient Manor of Purpoole in Holborn'[54]. It included a dovehouse, windmill, garden and 30 acres of arable land. By 1300 he started to take in law students, and seventy years later there was business there for eleven shops.

When the Knights Templar were suppressed in 1312 their property near the Round Church passed to the Knights Hospitallers, who leased part of it to lawyers for use as a hostel. It has remained a home for lawyers, developing into the Inner and Middle Temples, the Benchers obtaining ownership in 1609.

King's Justices set up households at Inner and Middle Temple, Lincoln's Inn and Gray's Inn. As Inns of Court they became the heart of the new legal system, and later the homes of the barristers' societies in England and Wales.

The term 'barrister' refers to a 'bar', reflecting the real or imaginary partition separating the bench and the front row of counsels' seats from the rest of the court and the public. The 'utter' (outer) barristers and public remain outside the 'bar'. The grassy hill thus became the home of two quite different kinds of 'bar'.

## § 3.6 INNS OF CHANCERY AS MEDIEVAL LAW SCHOOLS

The new legal system developed through rigidly standardised, recorded forms of action. Legal proceedings had to comply with a small number of forms of Writ, issued from the Royal Chancery – ('Chancery' from 'Chancellery', the Lord Chancellor's Department). For legal practitioners and Court staff knowledge of the Royal Chancery procedures was vital. The Inns of Chancery were established to teach it.

The Inns of Chancery provided preparatory training for those wishing to become barristers, training for those wishing to become attorneys (solicitors), and training for work in the Royal Courts. They were medieval law schools, giving a basic training in legal practice. Each became a 'daughter' body of an Inn of Court, which for a period provided trusteeship and educational supervision.

In the English language of the day, 'Inn' meant simply a house, residence or dwelling place. It was a place to be in. To contrast today's more common meaning, these Inns never earned their living through the sale of alcohol and meals to the public. (That is not to deny, however, that enough alcohol has been consumed in Staple Inn over the centuries to float many battleships, and indeed it is claimed that there was once a public house there – see section 4.5.)

# CHAPTER FOUR
## *The Society of Staple Inn, and Inn of Chancery, 1400–1580*

### § 4.1 BIRTH OF THE SOCIETY OF STAPLE INN AND THE INN OF CHANCERY, 1400–1415

The disappearance of the wool trade from *le Stapled Halle* by about 1375 coincided with the growing need for legal trainees for the expanding royal justice system. Its location near Chancery Lane, and the experience of law merchants there, made the site a 'natural' for an Inn of Chancery. Lawyers took up residence between 1378 and 1400, and became established there by 1415 as 'The Grand Company and Fellows of Staple Inn', or the 'Society of Staple Inn'.

The founding Principal and governing body of Ancients (Grandfellows) needed an appropriate title for their new Society. The link with the wool trade readily provided it, and 'Staple Inn' was born, the first Inn of Chancery.

### § 4.2 STAPLE INN LINKED TO GRAY'S INN

Staple Inn was conveniently close to the Inns of Court at both Gray's Inn and Lincoln's Inn, and soon became a 'daughter' body of Gray's Inn. The connection was formalised in 1529 when the Benchers of Gray's Inn purchased the land on which Staple Inn stood, although no rent was ever charged.

Gray's Inn 'acquired' a second Inn of Chancery 130 metres from Staple Inn down Holborn road towards the City, at Barnard's Inn, established in 1439. Barnard's and Staple Inns are unique among the Inns of Chancery in surviving physically today. Both are still occupied by professional and educational bodies – Barnard's Inn by Gresham College.

The formal relationship between the various Inns was recorded as late as 1631 by an Order in Council which declared that 'the Inns of Chancery shall hold their government subordinate to the Benchers of the Inns of Court to which they belong', and 'that the Benchers of every Inn of Court cause the Inns of Chancery to be surveyed, that there may be a competent number of Chambers for Students'[55].

Each term Gray's Inn offered Staple Inn a choice of three barristers from whom to choose a Reader, responsible for teaching and supervising the students' education. In other respects the Gray's Inn Benchers acted as trustees, avoiding close involvement in the day-to-day running of Staple Inn. This spared them much argument with the Staple Inn Ancients, who jealously guarded considerable freedom to run their own affairs.

### § 4.3 MEMBERSHIP OF THE SOCIETY OF STAPLE INN

The Society of Staple Inn was governed by a Principal, elected for three years, a Pensioner (responsible for money), and eight to eleven Ancients or Grandfellows.

The Society opened its membership to some who were not lawyers but who could bring money and status. Wool merchants were prominent through their historical association with the place and their wealth. Some became Principals. Wool merchants owned the land at Staple Inn for long periods. Robert Warner, wool-stapler, acquired it in 1407, and for the next hundred years it passed to other members of his family.

The Ancients made Staple Inn their London home. They rented out rooms for students and other lawyers' chambers. Dining and teaching took place in the Hall.

### § 4.4 STUDENTS AT STAPLE INN

For students, attendance at an Inn of Chancery was the contemporary version of university or 'finishing school', before moving on to the serious business of earning a living. By no means were all thirsting for a legal life. Sir John Fortescue wrote in the fifteenth century that:

> for the endowment of vertue and abandoning of vice, Knights, Barons with other states and noblemen of the Realm place their children in those Inns though they desire not to have them learned in the Laws nor to live by the practice thereof[58].

The combination of students with their minds on other matters and lecturers untrained in teaching must have given rise to some interesting incidents in 'class'. One of the matters on the students' minds might have been the length of their or their friends' beards, which were the subject of legislation in the sixteenth century. Their growth was not to exceed three weeks in term, with a 40 shilling fine, doubled every week for non-compliance. It has been suggested that the subtlety of legal minds in dealing with this imposition on personal freedom brought into our language the phrase 'splitting hairs'.

Edmund Bunny (1540–1618) was a student at Staple Inn in 1560–1561 before moving to Gray's Inn. He was a free spirit, defying his father who wished a legal career for him and disinherited him when he insisted on going into the church. He became a well-known itinerant preacher, and has a monument in York Minster.

Barnabe Googe (1540–1594) of Lincolnshire came to Staple Inn by age 20 for a year or two after uncompleted study at both Cambridge and Oxford. He married soon afterwards, thanks to help from Lord Cecil who persuaded Archbishop Parker to authorise his betrothal to a girl whose parents claimed was already betrothed to a rich landowner. The marriage appears to have succeeded as they had eight children. He became a highly esteemed and prolific writer and translator.

By contrast and much less successful was Timothy Kendall from Oxfordshire, a student at Staple Inn from 1577 after leaving Oxford University without a degree. He was a verse-writer and the compiler of *Flowers of Epigrammes*, but the *Dictionary of National Biography* reports that 'few of the translated epigrams have any merit and some are grotesquely bad'. His claim to fame seems to be that he was very poor!

Legal instruction was mainly through simulated court hearings and case studies, (elegantly titled 'moots' and 'bolts'), listening to 'readings', and supervision by the Gray's Inn Reader. The moots often took place during the day, the more advanced Grand moots often after dinner in the evening. Then the trainees were given no notice of the case to be argued, the prepared text being laid on the main salt cellar during the meal, tantalisingly unreadable. The readings, or lectures, also often delivered after dinner in the Hall, were solid affairs, and had sufficient authority to be quoted elsewhere. Private study was difficult as books were scarce, but no doubt some attempted it.

If the teaching methods seem quaint, it may be argued that they are an early form of the case-study approach to learning adopted successfully for many years, and still today, by the Harvard Business School in America.

§ 4.5 SOCIETY OF STAPLE INN BUILDINGS AND SETTING, 1400–1580

We know little about the buildings at the start of this new enterprise. Presumably there was an early phase of adapting the trading, stabling and storage buildings

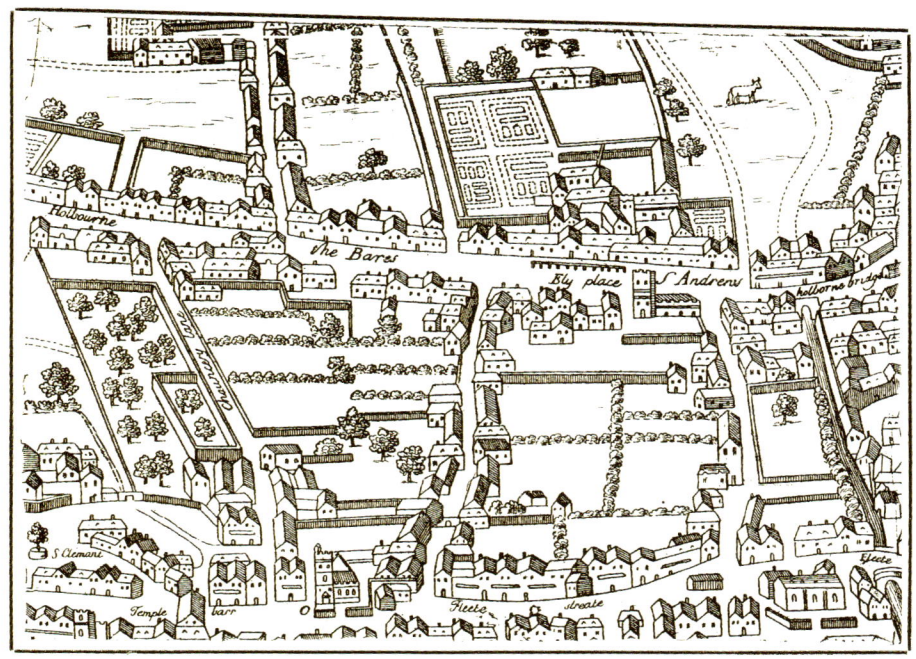

*Staple Inn and its surroundings, 1560.*
Adapted from Ralph Agas' map circa 1560-1570 for T. Cato Worsfold, 1903.
(© Henry Bumpus, publisher)

for use by the legal fraternity. The existence of high quality stained glass in the hall suggests a degree of splendour. A notice in the 'Cittie of York' public house today across the Holborn road by the entrance to Gray's Inn suggests also that there was a good social life[7]. It claims that it is named after a pub which used to be in Staple Inn in the sixteenth century – if true that was probably before the 1580s buildings were constructed along the road front, closing off the courtyard.

The immediate setting was attractive. The Braun and Hogenberg *Atlas of London* (1572) shows the area in about 1560[6], 150 years after the Society's start. Fields, trees and terraces stretch south down the hill from Staple Inn to the Thames, past houses on the country lane at Fleet Street. To the north of the Holborn road there were a few great houses of noblemen with orchards, cattle meadows, brooks, watermills, and pleasant gardens with roses, shaded by oak, willow and elm trees. Within a few hundred yards to the east on the Holborn road were other Inns of Chancery; Furnival's Inn with law students from about 1400, Barnard's Inn from soon after 1439, and Thavie's Inn from before 1422. To the west there were open fields for 1,300 metres to St Giles-in-the-Fields, near today's New Oxford Street, with a hospital for 40 lepers founded in 1101, and adapted in 1354 for use by the poor. This was a lovely, prosperous, fertile country setting.

§ 4.6 MIDDLE ROW'S SHADOW OVER STAPLE INN, FROM ABOUT 1500

Less attractive was the Middle Row building in the road outside Staple Inn.

The Holborn Bars were at a wide point in the Holborn road near the junction with Gray's Inn road. As noted in section 2.6 the early traders stopped and camped in the road outside the Bars, but after 1270 *le Stapled Halle* was available. A map of 1313 derived by E. Williams shows no buildings on the road outside the Bars[55].

Buildings appear in the road in a 1520 map. Some time after *le Stapled Halle* changed its use to an Inn of Chancery more business and residential premises were needed near the Bars. The Middle Row building was probably first built, (with possible additions later), between 1450 and 1500 to support the growing

*The shadow of Middle Row over Staple Inn.*
Engraving by Samuel Rawle for W. Herbert, 1804. (© Institute of Actuaries Library)

activity at Gray's, Staple, Furnival's, Barnard's and Thavie's Inns nearby, with their need for shops and lodgings. The students and lawyers were moneyed people with strong needs to satisfy. The early development of retailing took place in areas such as this.

Throughout its 350 to 400 years Middle Row had shops on the ground floor and stores and lodgings on the higher floors. A 1520 map shows 24 houses in the block[45]. There are reports of comb makers, cutlers, brokers, and a lottery office. By the 1720s it was famous for its wigmakers.

A 1560 map confirms the Middle Row buildings[1], with the Staple Inn buildings still set back some way from the road. Middle Row was built long before Staple Inn's Elizabethan black-and-white half-timbered buildings on the Holborn road frontage.

For most of its 200 feet length Middle Row was only 10 to 13 feet from the buildings on the south side of the Holborn road. The overhanging gables of the two sets of buildings nearly met. Although the east end of Middle Row, covering the full width of the junction with Gray's Inn road, only just reached the west end of Staple Inn's 1589 buildings, so that they did not overlap, it nevertheless dominated the approach to Staple Inn. It also severely impeded traffic along those busy roads (Gray's Inn road being the route from the north to the City's markets), adding to the disturbance, noise and complaint for local people and traders. Charles Dickens refers unflatteringly to the impact of Middle Row on Staple Inn in *The Mystery of Edwin Drood*. (See section 7.6.)

§ 4.7 OUTSIDE THE PARISH

In common with other Inns of Chancery, Staple Inn was ex-parochial. It was not formally beholden to St Andrew's Church down the road to the east, nor were its inhabitants compelled to attend a parish church when James I ordered parishioners to do so. Nevertheless the members of Staple Inn, as other Inns of Chancery nearby, regarded St Andrew's with affection, contributed money to its upkeep, and had the use of a chapel and some pews there for several centuries. It is said that following the election of a new Principal, members of Staple Inn took tea and coffee in the Hall, offered their congratulations, and processed to St Andrew's Church clad in gowns and holding nosegays – (which had utility beyond their decorous appearance against the stench of the market place and the Fleet nearby)[58].

Traditionally on Ascension Day Staple Inn's doors were closed to prevent parishioners 'beating the bounds' and thus including the Inn within the parish.

§ 4.8 THE SCENE TOWARDS THE CITY UNTIL 1580

A short distance beyond St. Andrew's Church was St. Bartholomew's Hospital, the oldest in London, founded in 1123. It was next to the Smithfield (the smooth field) horse market. Originally the hospital was built in fields, but the area deteriorated through the industry of butchers, tanners, brewers, tilers, cutlers and other businesses growing there from the thirteenth century. Piles of rotting, stinking waste accumulated in the Fleet. Worse still, the City's waste had for long been dumped as huge 'laystalls' of rubbish between the walls and the Fleet, adding to the desolation and stench of the area. The scavengers, whose job it was to clear the debris, often worked conscientiously on this task for their parishes, and were aided unofficially by many kites and crows, but the backlogs of debris could not be cleared. The magic of double-time pay at weekends and extra pairs of hands came in a much later century.

Much of this desolation was only a few hundred yards from Staple Inn. With an east wind the smell must have been oppressive. In 1440 there was a riot when law students confronted the butchers who cleaned carcasses in the Fleet.

Other problems afflicted the area. Violence, fire and excessive drink were regular concerns. London's first prison, the Fleet, had been built only 600 yards from the future Staple Inn early in the twelfth century. Known as 'the Gaol of London', it had a large moat filled with the usual collection of rubbish, topped up by latrines built over it. Graded accommodation was provided for prisoners on the 'ability to pay' principle (bribing the jailers), which may seem slightly odd since most prisoners were sent there as debtors.

The contrast between squalor and affluence was enormous. In 1531 Henry VIII and Catherine of Aragon attended a series of banquets over five days at Ely Place. The menu included 100 sheep, 51 cows, 91 pigs, 24 oxen, 720 chickens, 444 pigeons, 168 swans and over 4,000 larks. (Were any residents of Staple Inn invited to join in?)

Nearby, there were for many years gallows at each end of Fetter Lane, providing a rougher form of justice than that offered by the Inn's lawyers.

§ 4.9 THE ROAD TO TYBURN, FROM 1388

As Holborn road expanded its coaching and trade traffic it also became the scene for regular public entertainment. In 1388 gallows for public hangings were set up at Tyburn on Watling Street. The plaque marking this is at Marble Arch at the junction of the Bayswater and Edgware Roads. It became the main place for public executions until 1783.

Prisoners condemned to die were taken in a cart from Newgate to Tyburn on the road past Staple Inn. Others condemned to whipping were compelled to walk until their strength gave out, and were then dragged on a sledge, as was Titus Oates in 1685. Some were robust to the end – one man in 1753 'behaved with shocking impudence and unconcern and espying a woman who he knew, in a window in Holborn, used very obscene language to her'[36].

Many tried to look their best for the occasion, for occasion it was. They were aided by gifts from friends and the curious who came 'to take their last farewell and present them with white caps, with black ribbons, prayer books, nosegays and oranges that they may make a decent appearance up Holborn'[36]. 3,000 people called on McLean, a highwayman, in the death cell in about 1730 – a bonanza for the gaolers who charged for entry. In 1760 the eccentric murderer Lord Ferrers travelled the three-hour journey to his hanging through massive crowds from the Tower to Tyburn in his own landau in his wedding clothes. He was followed by a procession of friends and dignitaries in at least a dozen coaches.

There is much romantic writing about the nosegays of flowers given to the condemned (by prostitutes) at the gates of St Sepulchres as they left Newgate, the bell-ringing and chanting, and the last mug of ale provided at St Giles-in-the-Fields. Polly in *The Beggar's Opera* of 1728 by John Gay (1685–1732) refers to the 'volleys of sighs from the windows of Holborn' as Captain Macheath passes on his way to Tyburn[58]. In *Love for Love* of 1695 by William Congreve (1670–1729), Sir Sampson exclaims, 'Sirrah, you will be hanged, I shall live to see you go up Holborn Hill'[58]. Jonathan Swift wrote a long poem in similar spirit, including:

> As clever Tom Clinch, while the rabble was bawling,
> Rode stately through Holborn, to die in his calling;
> He stopt at the George for a bottle of sack,
> And promis'd to pay for it when he'd came back.[58]

Hanging days were public holidays, supposedly to discourage bad behaviour through public example. However they were much less a deterrent than entertainment. Londoners were all too accustomed to death and its public and formal ritual in the streets. London's sights included victims' heads impaled on iron spikes above the main gateway of London Bridge and above Temple Bar.

Spyglasses and telescopes were available at a modest charge. Huge crowds (on one occasion in 1724 allegedly as many as 200,000 for Jack Shepherd, the popular twenty-three-year old escapologist highwayman) attended the journey to Tyburn and milled around near the gallows enjoying a good day out. They saw friends and relatives tug at the hanging men's feet to speed death; others rush to seek supposed cure of disease from touching the dead bodies; and yet others struggle for possession for return to relatives – or for transport to surgeons for dissection. There were grandstand seats for the wealthy. And the crowds, men and women together, ensured that the children had a good view.

This continued until 1783, when the newly fashionable West End objected to the processions and unruly crowds, and the hangings returned to Newgate prison. The last public hanging there was in 1868.

§ 4.10 THE SOCIETY ADOPTS THE WOOLSACK INSIGNIA, ABOUT 1553

In stark contrast to that rough world, corporations and societies began to assume the privilege of bearing coats of arms – heraldic devices or shields – from about the mid sixteenth century. The arms of the Inner Temple are shown in a woodcut in a 1563 book[33]. The 1553 reference, with the woolsack insignia, on the Mace of the Society of Staple Inn (see section 9.5) may date the Society's formal adoption of the woolsack. Sir George Buck reported the Arms' existence in 1615[47].

The Society's insignia show a silver woolsack on a green field. Presumably it was selected for the same reason as the Society's choice of its own title, the association of the place with the wool trade and merchant law. The woolsack symbol was probably used at Staple Inn from the formation of the Society.

There is a woolsack in stone over the entrance to the Hall from the courtyard, a gilded woolsack on the iron gates leading to Chancery Lane, and there are woolsacks on the gates into the garden from Southampton Buildings. The symbol was on pewter and china used in the Hall.

Not linked with the Society of Staple Inn, the Company of the Merchants of the Staple was granted arms with no woolsack, and the Woolmen's Company has a woolsack with red background.

THE SOCIETY OF STAPLE INN, AND INN OF CHANCERY

*The execution of Lord Ferrers, 1760.* (© The British Museum)

# CHAPTER FIVE
# Staple Inn 1580–1700: From Prosperity to Difficulty

## § 5.1 MAJOR REBUILDING, 1580–1592

The growing independence of Staple Inn from Gray's Inn was exemplified in the great rebuilding of 1580–1592. (Gray's Inn had been rebuilt in 1556–1560.)

These were tough times. Life was 'solitary, poor, nasty, brutish and short' for many, as Thomas Hobbes (1588–1679) famously wrote, perhaps from his one-time home in Fetter Lane. Plague and other epidemics took severe toll. 1563, for instance, was a bad plague year when a quarter of Londoners died. In 1574 Francis Bacon's law studies at Cambridge were interrupted by plague, and he left without a degree. Plague raged in London in 1581, as the main Hall construction was being completed.

Life was also robust. London's population quadrupled from 50,000 in 1500 to 200,000 in 1600. It expanded by two-and-a-half times from 1565–1600. The number of baptisms at St Andrew's Church trebled from the 1560s to the 1590s. The growth of central government, London's attractions to the gentry, and the expansion of trade all contributed to the population explosion. There was rising secular confidence in prosperous Elizabethan England in the wake of the Reformation.

The demands on the legal profession grew. Pleas at King's Bench increased tenfold in the sixteenth century. The success of Staple Inn led to overcrowding and the need for a substantial rebuild. Part of the east side had been built in 1530–1545, but by the late sixteenth century some structures on the site, including the Hall, had stood for nearly 300 years. Ignoring the dire religious judgements which many Catholics and Protestants alike were attributing to the earthquake which struck London on 6 April 1580, Staple Inn's Ancients decided to modernise and expand their business.

*The coat-of-arms of Richard Champion, Principal of the Society of Staple Inn and sponsor of the new Staple Inn Hall built in 1581. The crest was restored in 1996.*
*(Staple Inn Hall © Prudential Corporation plc)*

### The Hall

With financial backing from the Principal, Richard Champion, and subscription from the Ancients, the land by the old Hall was purchased and a new, more splendid Hall was built in 1580–1581, where today's Hall stands. An entrance room with buttery above and nine chambers nearby were added in 1586.

The design of the new Hall followed that of many Oxbridge Colleges. A passage ran from the courtyard to the garden across the end of the Hall, with the kitchen on its other side. The kitchen had a traditional roasting bar, and cellars below. The gallery in the Hall above the passage was accessible only with the uncertain aid of a ladder. Philip Johnston suggests there is a strong resemblance between the screen supporting the gallery and that at Cuckfield Park, Sussex[31].

Notable features of the Hall included the louvre with stained glass panes, lead cupola and weathervane; the cupola bell tower, in which the bell later carried the name of Thomas Leech, Principal from 1753 to 1759; the stained glass windows; and the carved hammer-beam roof.

The classic simple hammer-beam roof has not only the common ornamental stalactite pendants but also 20 very unusual stalagmites standing on the hammers and collar beams. Let us enjoy their mystery, since no one can interpret them with conviction. Richard Champion presumably donated the roof, since his arms are carved on the corbel over the oriel window. Its side elevation records '1581' and 'R.C.' in picturesque style – but is hard to read from floor level. His arms are also displayed, without name, in a stained glass window near the courtyard entrance. The wainscot was given in 1589 by Robert Willett, Principal, and the interior was finished in 1592.

The Hall was heated by an open fire or brazier in the middle of the floor below the louvre in the roof far above. The smoke was supposed to escape through this, and no doubt some did. However inhalation of the smoky air by those dining or taking part in discussions must have added a significant dimension to their legal and social activity.

There were rushes on the floor, which were changed but once each term. For ceremonial occasions the Society's mace was placed on a flat structure towards the end of the Hall – a 'cupboard', or board on which to place cups, with storage below. There were probably three dining tables, one each for the Ancients, the barristers and superior students, and the 'varlets and clerks'[33]. The latter paid lower admission fees and in return waited on those at the high table. Each table formed a separate 'mess', but the whole Society dined together.

The natural, light colour of the oak throughout the Hall, offsetting the colours in the stained glass, must have achieved a wonderful sense of fresh, new beginning for the lawyers and their wealthy friends and patrons.

*New buildings on the Holborn road frontage and other houses*
Most significantly for London's future architectural history – and for Staple Inn's own long-term survival – new shops and houses were built in 1586–1589 on the open ground on Holborn road frontage. These are described by Simon Bradley and Nikolaus Pevsner as 'the most impressive surviving example in London of a long and high group of Elizabethan half-timbered houses'[5]. The range contains seven façade gables, in two groups. The two gables to the west, built in 1589, are of a different design, slightly taller, and until 1936 with different floor levels from the five to the east, which were built by Vincent Engham in 1586. The latter contain a central freestone archway and larger oriel window gracing the entrance to the courtyard, with two symmetrical oriel windows on each side to the upper storey below the gable. The full-width attic casements above are rare, and possibly unique in the south-east of England. These houses provided one-room ground-floor shops along the front, and rear access to the chambers above. If there was a public house on the site before this work (see section 4.5) it would have gone with the 'closure' of the courtyard from the road by the new buildings.

Principal Vincent Engham rebuilt the houses on the west of the courtyard in the mid-1580s. Nos. 9 and 10 were added in 1597 on the site of the old Hall.

Some houses were funded in exchange for rooms, since this was an attractive residential site; others were on a building lease with reversion later to the Society. Some owners passed their house through several generations of the family before reversion to the Society.

Many students and residents would have found the new ambience of Staple Inn agreeably like the high quality homes in the country from which they had come. They might even have been accustomed to stained glass in windows.

§ 5.2 STAINED GLASS IN THE HALL, 1581–1618
Some stained glass may have been transferred from the old Hall to the new in the two unnamed panels in the lower middle sections of the second and third windows on the south side and in the 'Nicholas Brokus' panel in the north window near the courtyard entrance. They seem to be composite constructions including some pieces from high-quality windows possibly made earlier than 1581 and other pieces made later. One of the unnamed panels contains a Tudor rose and a merchant's mark of an equilateral triangle (for a woolmonger?) and also a shield bearing parts of the Pope family coat of arms. Thomas Pope had been a 'continuer' in 1585. The same Pope coat also features above another on the other unnamed south window, which also includes a fragment from the name

## CHAPTER FIVE

'Mansel'. Robert Mansell was Principal in 1584. Recent research dates the presence of the Mansell arms before 1595 but the Pope coat is not noted until 1661 and is not included in early descriptions of other arms in the Hall.

The four upper panels in the north wall window near the courtyard entrance display the arms of four men likely to have been the main benefactors of the 1581 Hall. They are Nicholas Brocket ('Brokus' as it appears on the glass), Principal in 1543, who had died in 1585; Richard Champion, Principal from 1580 to 1583; Charles Bagehot, continuer in 1585; and Thomas Trayle. The four panels are of similar style with matching surrounds to their crests. They appear to date from 1580 to 1585, but only the Brocket and Bagehot panels are noted in the 1595 manuscript description.

Soon six more stained glass panels were added – among the finest glass in London. The three panels in the top row of the first south window, near the dais, contain the royal arms of Elizabeth I, James I, and the Prince of Wales, then aged 18, the future Charles I. In the middle row are the arms of three judges from the reign of James I. It is possible that the Elizabeth panel was included when the Hall was built, and the James I panel any time from 1603 when he became King. It is a reasonable guess that Sir Thomas Walmesley's panel was installed when he died in 1612, and the other three in 1618, the date on their panels.

Sir Richard Hutton (1561?–1639) from Cumberland was at Staple Inn from 1579 to 1580, after studying divinity at Cambridge, where he was at some risk of arrest as an alleged papist. He moved to Gray's Inn in 1580. In 1603 he was elected

*Early stained glass in Staple Inn Hall bearing mark of merchant trade and crest fragments associated with Thomas Pope and Robert Mansel.*
(Staple Inn Hall © Prudential Corporation plc)

*Windows of Elizabeth I, James I and Charles I as Prince of Wales.*
(Staple Inn Hall © Prudential Corporation plc)

Gray's Inn Reader, but an outbreak of plague deprived him of students. He was knighted in 1617, and was one of four judges granted control of Sir Francis Bacon's £40,000 fine for alleged bribery. In 1638, having previously given his opinion in favour of ship money in the interests of conformity with other judges, he publicly changed his mind and judged it illegal – and won £50,000 damages from a high church clergyman who accused him of treason. Charles I had revived and greatly expanded this previously occasional tax without Parliament's approval.

Thomas Walmesley (1537–1612) from Lancashire may never have resided at Staple Inn. It is unclear whether he started at Staple Inn, Barnard's Inn, or went straight to Lincoln's Inn in 1559, to become a barrister and in 1589 a Judge of the Common Pleas. He, too, before election as serjeant was under suspicion of papist tendencies. This was an era of acute religious sensitivities. He was knighted in 1603.

Sir Peter Warburton (1540?–1621) was a member of Staple Inn for a year or two before moving to Lincoln's Inn in 1562, becoming a barrister there in 1572, a sheriff and M.P. in his native Cheshire, and a Justice of the Common Pleas from 1600 to 1621. He was involved in the trials of Walter Raleigh in 1603 and of the gunpowder plotters in 1605. He was knighted in 1603.

The judges all had distinguished careers, but none was Principal at Staple Inn. So why the investment in these six splendid panels of royalty and judges? The answer may simply be that the Society wished to raise its status and prestige in

*Windows of Sir Richard Hutton, Thomas Walmesley, Sir Peter Warburton... 'among the finest glass in London'.*
(Staple Inn Hall © Prudential Corporation plc)

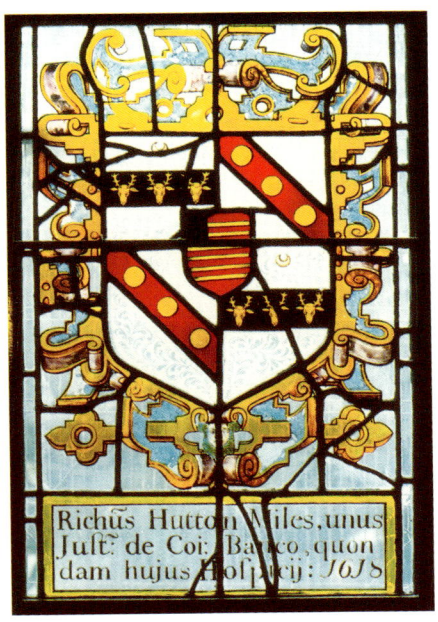
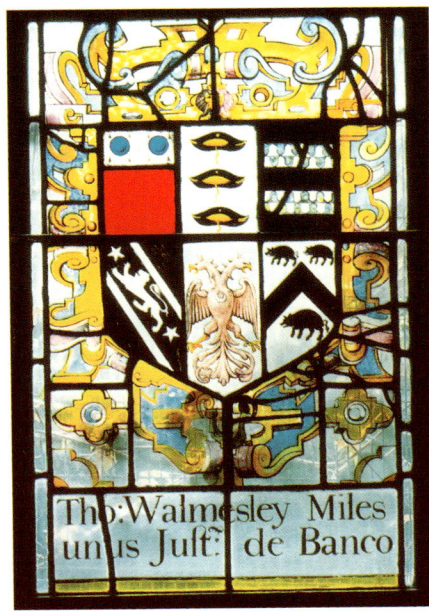
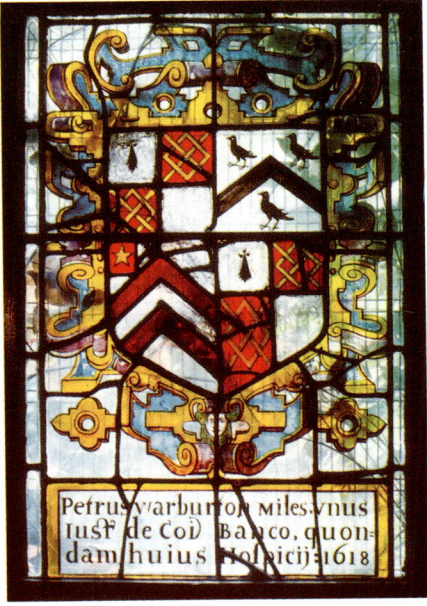

its new Hall. The royal panels would have been presented as a patriotic gesture. The judges were all Judges of Common Pleas – eminent men in the field of law closest to the work at Staple Inn. (Common law procedures tend to maximise the role of advocates and depend heavily on case law, responding to specific cases, less to legal theorising as in civil law.) These were men of high status and prestige in the world in which the Society of Staple Inn was operating.

That such patriotic gestures were fashionable is suggested by 'Prince Henry's Room', built at No. 17 Fleet Street over the Inner Temple Gatehouse in 1610 to 1611. On the ceiling of this splendid oak-panelled room were the three feathers of the Prince of Wales together with the inscription 'P.H.', in honour of the new Prince of Wales, son of James I.

The moves by the Society to raise its status and prestige also reflected its growing independence from Gray's Inn. In 1584, when the new Hall was still being fitted out, the Readers of Gray's Inn petitioned that Thomas Cary should be elected Staple Inn Principal to succeed Reginald Knight who had died. The Ancients of Staple Inn thought otherwise, electing another Gray's Inn member, Robert Mansell. He was succeeded a year later by Vincent Engham who did not belong to Gray's Inn.

It took a major incident, such as unruly disturbances at Staple Inn in 1596, for Gray's Inn to act decisively. They then removed the Staple Inn Principal despite the Ancients' objections, appointing in his place a Mr Champion, who was presumably the Principal who had been so instrumental in the rebuilding of the Hall in 1581. It seems that on this occasion the Staple Inn Ancients had lost the confidence of their students, so that 'outside' help could not be rejected easily.

Thereafter Gray's Inn's influence over Staple Inn gradually declined. No Gray's Inn Readers were appointed after 1675. There were social and symbolic activities linking the two Inns, and no doubt many personal friendships and working relationships between their members. In general, however, the governing body of Staple Inn was able to direct and manage its own affairs as it saw fit. Only five of the 51 known Principals of Staple Inn from 1580 to 1884 were also members of Gray's Inn.

## § 5.3 'THE FAYREST INNE OF CHAUNCERY IN THIS UNIVERSITIE', 1615

An account in 1615 by Sir George Buck gives Staple Inn the accolade by which it is often described, and suggests some success by the Society in promoting the Inn:

> Staple Inn was the Inne or Hostell of the Merchants of the Staple (as the tradition is), wherewith until I can learne better matter, concerning the antiquity and foundation thereof, I must rest satisfied. But for latter matters I cannot chuse but make report, and much to the commendation of the Gentlemen of this House, that they have bestowed great costs in new-building a fayre Hall of brick, and two parts of the outward Courtyards, besides other lodging in the garden and elsewhere, and have thereby made it the fayrest Inne of Chauncery in this Universitie[47].

## § 5.4 LOOKING FOR THE OLD BOURNE: THE MAGIC OF THE WATER

Charles Dickens refers in 1870 to the Staple Inn buildings overlooking the public way 'as if disconsolately looking for the Old Bourne which has long run dry'[15]. When first built they would have overlooked a ditch or gulley along each side of the broad road outside, with no pavements. Most roads at that time were made to slope to the centre to drain water, but wide roads such as through Holborn often had gulleys on each side.

Apart from repaving in 1417 and 1535, the Holborn road was hardly maintained for centuries. Holborn householders' formal obligation to light, clean and repair their streets was not followed with any enthusiasm at all. Water from springs in the area will have helped rainwater to keep the gulleys flowing down the hill to the Fleet for part of the year despite the debris and lack of care. Such water was plentiful. Some houses in Fetter Lane were later found to have been built over arches with fine river sand below. The Prudential surveyor reported that work on his headquarters building in 1939 was handicapped by water ten feet deep in the ground[8]. Such refuse as did not escape along the gullies had some chance of being collected by the night cart (or perhaps by keen gardeners, including surely those from Staple Inn, collecting the offerings of the horses on the roadway).

In common with many large houses, Staple Inn had no need to tap the distant and less hygienic water supplies brought to the City by pipes from the thirteenth century. Its springs feeding the well and pump in the courtyard were believed to produce pure water with medicinal qualities. When centuries later the courtyard pump was detached from the well and connected to the London Metropolitan Water Company pipe the medicinal qualities of the water were still acclaimed. The impact of nearby cesspools is unclear.

### § 5.5 INHABITANTS OF STAPLE INN FROM THE 1550S TO 1700

Half the freehold space at Staple Inn was occupied by Fellows of the Society. Other rooms were occupied by tenants, some of whom had already qualified for election as Fellows, some with the right to become Fellows in future. The Hall was funded by Fellows' subscriptions, the houses through private commercial enterprise.

The lawyers and other people who were attracted to live and work at Staple Inn were mainly from the privileged classes. So also were the students. Most were sent by leading, sometimes aristocratic, families from other parts of the country to experience the London scene and to acquire a useful qualification. The upper classes applied an effective 'closed shop' for entry to the legal profession.

A 1586 census showed that Staple Inn had more students than any other Inn of Chancery[55], with 145 in term and 69 in the vacations – 23% and 32% respectively of all students at the Inns of Chancery. Barnard's Inn was next in number with 112, whilst Thavie's Inn had only 40. In comparison Gray's Inn had 356 students in term and 229 in vacation, 37% and 57% respectively of the total numbers at the four Inns of Court.

It is inconceivable that as many as 145 students lodged at Staple Inn in 1586 as well as the qualified lawyers and others living there. Some lived in lodgings nearby, including very likely Middle Row in the Holborn road outside.

After a year or two successful candidates who still wished to pursue that career moved on to Gray's Inn or to one of the other Inns of Court for more advanced tuition and experience. Four or five years later they might be called to the bar as junior barristers, the passing out process being the 'general consent' of Benchers and Readers. There were no written examinations in those days.

The number of students who went on to Gray's Inn from Staple Inn was small. The highest recorded annual contingent is 13 in 1570. The number had declined drastically a century later – only one between 1690 and 1746, 23 between 1746 and 1785, and none thereafter. Some Staple Inn students moved to other Inns of Court. Sir Thomas Walmesley went to Lincoln's Inn in 1559 aged 22 to qualify there as a barrister, as did Sir Peter Warburton a few years later.

Most legal students went direct from home to an Inn of Court without a preparatory spell at an Inn of Chancery. The four Inns of Court admitted 150 students annually during the 1560s, and as many as 280 in many years from 1610 to 1640, mainly direct from landed families. The place of the Inns of Chancery in the legal framework was far from secure.

Staple Inn had its share of characters. Sir Francis Crawley (1584–1649) of Leicestershire came to Staple Inn before moving to Gray's Inn in 1598 aged fourteen. A man with an eye to the main chance, he was impeached for backing the King's demand for the royal prerogative against Parliament. He supported the King in the Civil War. His progress through the legal profession was described by one of his contemporaries as 'that of a diligent spy through a country into which he meant to conduct an enemy'[16].

Robert Callis was a Gray's Inn barrister with, it seems, a highly developed sense of humour. He created dissension in the legal ranks through his work *The case and Argument against Sir Ignoramus of Cambridge*. He read his comedy of 'Ignoramus' at a meeting attended by King James in 1615, and again at a Reading in Staple Inn Hall in Lent 1616. It was described as a 'supposititious law case involving Ignoramus clerk illiteratus'[16]. Let us hope the students benefited from it. Later, Callis became Commissioner of Sewers in his native Lincolnshire.

Some students stayed at Staple Inn to qualify for legal work appropriate to an Inn of Chancery. Many others moved back to their homes or elsewhere in the country to pursue careers looking after their estates, or in law or other walks of life. These were litigious times, and a landlord needed to know the law to preserve his property. From the sixteenth to eighteenth centuries more English county families were founded by lawyers than by members of the cloth trade.

The garden at Staple Inn provided a touch of country life for residents. According to the *Prudential Bulletin*, John Gerard (1545–1612), herbalist and barber-surgeon, rented it to grow some of the rare plants which he, sponsors and friends collected from many countries[40]. He recorded more than one thousand species in *The Herball*, or *General Histoire of Plantes* (1597), the first plant catalogue.

## § 5.6 LIFE AT STAPLE INN IN THE LATE SIXTEENTH AND SEVENTEENTH CENTURIES

In addition to their legal training students at Staple Inn learned singing, dancing and other aids to noble living. Some put more energy into wider aspects of life than into the law. Social and intellectual life at Staple Inn was pleasant, similar to and more comfortable than that at an Oxbridge College, with better accommodation, food and drink, and more scope for pastimes such as drama and dancing. The inhabitants of Staple Inn had the opportunity to enjoy the active lifestyle of the relatively wealthy, and to patronise the growing range of cultural and other entertainment that London offered. Holborn and the Strand became lively areas for gentlemen, stimulating intellectual life and luxury trades.

There was a huge change in social behaviour following the dissolution of the monasteries. Between 1543 and 1547 twenty-three major religious houses in and near the City were taken over by the Crown. Most were sold on to wealthy private individuals to finance the royal wars against France and Scotland. As religion declined, so the attractions of the secular life came increasingly to the fore, at least for the well-to-do.

The Theatre and The Curtain theatres were built in 1576 and 1577 on the site of Holywell Priory, one and a half miles away in Shoreditch. The former was dismantled and rebuilt as the Globe Theatre in 1599 in the Bishop of Winchester's Clink Liberty in Southwark on the South bank. (This Liberty also housed eighteen brothels.) Among other new theatres the Blackfriars Theatre was opened in 1577, operating mainly in the winter when the Globe and Rose Theatres across the river were drowning in muddy water – their turn came in the summer. Typically these theatres had three levels of galleries around an unroofed yard with a raised stage and a standing area –see today's reconstructed Globe Theatre. (The original Globe Theatre was destroyed in 1613 when two cannon fired during *Henry VIII* set the thatch alight. It was rebuilt in 1614, closed by the Puritans in 1642, and demolished in 1644.)

Playwrights were prolific, including William Shakespeare (1564–1616), Christopher Marlowe (1564–1593), Ben Jonson (1572–1637) and Thomas Heywood (1574–1641) – the latter alone writing 220 plays. One impresario handled over 300 plays between 1592 and 1600. Even closer to home, Lincoln's Inn Fields Theatre opened from 1660 to 1732, before moving to New Covent Garden Theatre. John Dryden (1631–1700) lived for a time in Fetter Lane.

Theatre performances were usually in the afternoon daylight between 2.00 p.m. and 5.00 p.m. A wide range of humanity mingled together at them. Residents and students of Staple Inn would have attended these theatres regularly – and surely also the somewhat erratic first performance of *The Comedy of Errors* in Gray's Inn Hall in 1594.

A short walk from Staple Inn, the Thames offered both recreation and transport. Large numbers of watermen earned a living with taxis and pleasure boats. The river was narrower than in Roman days (when at high tide it had been one kilometre across near the site of London Bridge) but wider than today since most building over water and marshy banks came in the late nineteenth and twentieth centuries. The river was shallower and the current easier than today, but it was hugely more crowded with hazardous traffic.

One hazard was shooting the rapids under London Bridge. These were caused by the outgoing flood competing with the incoming tide below the bridge as it

*The Thames on Lord Mayor's Day showing numerous forms of transport.*
Antonio Canal, called Canaletto (1697–1768), circa 1746. (© AKG London Ltd)

'then with closed eyes, clench'd hands, and quick-drawn breath, darts at the central arch …'[26].

The watermen's service was often halted by winter weather. England's climate passed through a mini Ice Age during the sixteenth, seventeenth and eighteenth centuries, with temperatures several degrees lower on average than in the twentieth century. The Thames froze regularly in winter for many years. Walking, skating, and camping with bonfires on the ice were normal pursuits. The last frost fair took place as late as 1813–1814, and in 1820 the river froze to a depth of 5 feet in mid-January. The replacement of the old London Bridge in 1831 by one with five arches enabled the river to flow more freely, and with more salt water above the bridge at high tide, and therefore be less likely to freeze.

Road transport was improving. Hackney coaches (named after the French *haquenee* – an ambling nag) with two seats and two horses, offered a reasonably quick local taxi service from 1634. 300 were licensed in 1654, 700 by 1694, 1,000 in 1768, with Hatton Garden and Red Lion Square staging posts near Staple Inn.

*A Frost Fair on the Thames 1683–1684 taken near the Temple stairs.*
(© Historical Publications Ltd)

struggled to pass through the 19 narrow archways. Their stone foundations were periodically strengthened until they filled five-sixths of the river-bed by 1750. The effect was like a mill-race or the sluices of a dam, with a difference in water level of several feet in extreme conditions between the two sides of the bridge. This was a challenge for the young, not to be overlooked by some Staple Inn inhabitants as preparation for a good bolt or moot in the evening – a variation, perhaps, on today's white water rafting. Without casting aspersions on the latter, a contemporary quotation reports that 'London Bridge was made for wise men to go over and fools to go under'. George Canning's poem on the subject describes the technique of the 'venturous boatmen as down the steep fall the headlong waters go' and the 'dextrous steersman stops the veering helm', and

## CHAPTER FIVE

Sedan chairs offered reasonably private transport. For travel between Staple Inn and residents' country homes there were stagecoach bases at the White Horse at No. 90 Holborn with coaches for Oxford and the West Country, and at the Black Swan in Fetter Lane. This coaching house and hostelry advertised in 1706 a four-day journey to York, on offer three times each week – the caveat 'if God permits' a wise 'insurance' against complaints for late or failed delivery[58].

Games and sports available to the young men of Staple Inn included archery, ballgames, bowls, skittles, jumping and other athletics, wrestling, stone and javelin throwing, sailing, fishing, swimming, rowing, and skating. There were frequent Royal, State and City occasions to enjoy, and clubs, taverns and coffee houses to visit.

The London coffee house and tavern contributed to the growth of democracy, broadening the education of sections of society beyond clergy, lawyers and leading gentry. Within one hundred years of the opening of the first coffee house in St Michael's Alley off Cornhill in 1652 there were 551 in London providing opportunity for public debate and cultural exchange, and a similar number of taverns with private rooms. Newspapers and pamphlets were readily available to meet strong popular demand for news and opinion. Life at Staple Inn did not need to be closeted narrowly in the intricacies of the law, but could share in stimulating debate with other intelligent men as they sought to make sense of and influence the world around them.

Less salubrious to our eyes today were the popular sports of prize-fighting, baiting bears, badgers and bulls with fighting dogs, cock-fighting, and other unmentionable 'sports' with animals, often accompanied by winning and losing large sums of stake money. There were many gaming houses, including one reported in the *Gentleman's Magazine* 'by the little turnstile in Holebourne' as having been raided in 1752[36]. Consider Hogarth's print 'The Cockpit' of 1759, with James Boswell's comment – 'The uproar and the noise of betting is prodigious'[36]. Gentry and commoners mingled together. There was a cockpit just north of Gray's Inn. Lottery draws were public events with much publicity. From about 1600 to 1770 the Bethlehem Royal Hospital (Bedlam) on Moorfields offered its lunatic inmates as entertainment for the public, as people watch monkeys in a zoo today.

All these entertainments were readily accessible from Staple Inn. Samuel Pepys found 'a strange variety of people' from Members of Parliament to apprentices at a cock-fight in Shoe Lane in 1663[30]. This was early democracy at play, the wealthy rubbing shoulders without concern with those of much lesser means, often male and female equally.

The high spirits of the students, released from the rigours of a moot or reading, were noticed outside the Inn. In the seventeenth century the Star Chamber tried to exercise control by ordering the Inns to restrain those in their charge 'from being abroad from their houses after six of the clock at night, unless there are very grave and urgent cause'[58], and forbidding them from carrying weapons. One commentator reported frequent disturbances in the 1580s by reason of 'the unthrift of the Inns of Chancery', who were 'unruly on nights, walking about to the disturbance and danger of such as passed along the streets'[58]. 'Town and gown' tensions are not unique to today.

Another hazard for those walking near Staple Inn were the beggars, vagabonds and robbers who lay in wait for the unsuspecting. By early seventeenth century the area near Ely House (given by Elizabeth to Sir Christopher Hatton, thus breaking up the Bishop's estate) had deteriorated drastically, with highwaymen and stolen goods receivers prominent. Smithfield Market nearby was notorious for fighting and duelling, earning its popular name, 'Ruffians Hall'. Drovers enjoyed stampeding their cattle on the way to market, and if they did not young boys did it for them. The phrase 'a bull in a china shop' probably originates from unhappy cattle seeking refuge in houses and shops.

Although life was good for many well-to-do residents of Staple Inn it was very hard for the poor. Removal of the charitable services of monasteries and religious orders threw many of the weak on to the streets. Over-population, bad harvests, and decreasing real wages caused misery even for those with work, and led to civil unrest. There were food riots near Staple Inn in 1595. The poor were very poor indeed.

§ 5.7 IMPACT OF LONDON'S EXPANDING POPULATION, 1600–1700

London's population expanded rapidly from 200,000 in 1600 to 400,000 in 1650 and to nearly 600,000 in 1700[29]. The suburbs continued to behave with unbridled freedom in relation to the City. Numerous building regulations failed to stop new suburbs and buildings springing up all around London. The most dramatic expansions were in Holborn and Covent Garden. In 1632 there was a petition to the Privy Council against the 'multitude of newly erected tenements' in various places including Holborn and St Giles[29]. A 1638 list of 1,361 illicit London suburban houses included 404 in and near Holborn[29]. That area in particular experienced widening extremes of wealth and utter poverty and squalor.

Their extra-parochial status made the Inns of Court and of Chancery attractive havens to those seeking shelter or to escape authority. Seventeenth-century decrees sought to prevent sympathetic inhabitants of the Inns from harbouring such people, through regular searches of these 'privileged and exempted places'[58].

As the population grew buildings replaced gardens in and near the City. New market gardens sprang up in the surrounding countryside, in areas such as Knightsbridge and Chelsea to the west. Men did the farming, women the transporting, many past Staple Inn on their way to the City.

The streets were noisy and dirty. The grinding of wheels, many with iron rims, on cobbles and granite; the bumping of carts and the clattering of horses' hooves as they struggled through potholes, drains and loose stones in the road surface; the shouts of coachmen, hawkers and street vendors; the doubtful melodies of street musicians; the hubbub of passing crowds and animals; they all combined to produce noise effects far worse than today's. The regular winter fogs increased the need for warning sounds, and the frequency of accidents.

There were endless problems with hollowed elm water pipes under the roads. Probably in lengths of no more than seven feet, every joint was likely to leak, every breakage needed immediate attention, and pipes needed replacing every 20 years at best. Later, lead pipes were not much better. In cold weather horse-dung was placed over them for insulation.

Householders were expected to pave and maintain the street up to the centre line in front of their house, but few did so. A visitor warned against 'a loose stone in a pavement under which water lodges and on being trod upon squirts up, to the great detriment of white stockings'[36]. Such loose stones were known as 'beau-traps'.

The surface of Chancery Lane remained so bad that there were continuing efforts to close it as a hazard to life and limb. A simple walk along the roads in Holborn involved taking care to avoid the many potholes, signs swinging from buildings (there being no street numbering, and signs fixed to buildings not being required until 1760) and the erratic passage of horses and carts when they were not fuming in traffic jams – which Middle Row frequently caused. Henry Peacham (1576–1643) wrote in 1636:

> I have often observed the way barricado'd up with a coach, two, or three, that what haste, or business whatsoever a man hath, he must wait my Lady's (I know not whose) leisure (who is in the next shop buying pendants for her ears, or a collar for her dog) ere he can find any passage[26].

There were at least seventeen shops in Middle Row.

The discharge of chamber pots (curiously known as 'looking glasses') and refuse from windows overhead added to the hazard of vast volumes of excrement on the roads from horses, herds, flocks and dogs. Sharp antennae and agility were needed for successful passage. The air was increasingly acrid due to coal fires. And when it rained, according to the *Description of a City Shower* by Jonathan Swift (1667–1745):

> Now from all parts the swelling kennels flow,
> And bear their trophies with them as they go:
> Filth of all hues and odours seem to tell
> What street they'd sailed from by their sight and smell…
> and fall from their Conduit prone to Holborn Bridge[26].

# CHAPTER FIVE

'The Art of Walking the Streets of London' – showing some of the hazards in the late eighteenth century.

STAPLE INN 1580–1700

*How to stop up the Passage* — *How to make the most of the Mud*

*How to carry a Stick* — *How to get into the Watch-House*

The Art of Walking the Streets of London, Plate 2<sup>d</sup>.

Illustrations by George Woodward (1760–1809) engraved by George Cruikshank (1792–1878). (© Guildhall Library, Corporation of London)

There were violent disputes between pedestrians about who should 'take the wall' and walk furthest from the dangerous carts and their muddy splashes. Dr Johnson recorded in the eighteenth century a decline in these disputes through the introduction of a form of walkway etiquette or highway code:

> In the last age there were two sets of people, those who gave the wall, and those who took it; the peaceable and the quarrelsome… Now it is fixed that every man keeps to the right; or, if one is taking the wall, another yields it, and it is never a dispute[26].

Serious attempts to improve London's roads did not emerge until the 1760s.

Seventeenth century living conditions in Staple Inn were near to spartan, even after the Elizabethan inventions of the chimney and of improved bedding to aid warmth, comfort and sleep at night. They were, however, princely compared with the conditions of the slums that were taking root in the area.

## § 5.8 'CAVALIERS' OR 'ROUNDHEADS'?

The period of the Civil War from 1642 leading to the beheading in Whitehall of Charles I in 1649 and the military interregnum under Oliver Cromwell must have been difficult for Staple Inn's inhabitants. It is likely that some were firm Royalists, coming from noble families based in the country and naturally inclined by upbringing and profession to uphold a traditional view of the constitution and the law. One of the sons of the great judge Sir Richard Hutton was killed at Sherborne fighting for the King in the Civil War.

Others, including students, will have sided with the Puritans and City apprentices, some of whom were also from landed or merchant families, and who were a significant force for the public cause represented by Parliament. (Not necessarily significant yet interestingly, twentieth-century restoration work in Staple Inn found a four-page manuscript possibly from this period which was part of a treatise in the Presbyterian interest in favour of religious toleration[41].) Others probably tried to stay neutral, vacillated or changed views once or more, in common with merchants in the City who tended to lie low, with trade at a standstill. London, however, as many other towns, supported Parliament. Supplies of cloth, wool and coal to London were cut off by the Royalists. The cold winter months must have been hard to bear in Staple Inn, both physically and emotionally.

In autumn and winter 1642–1643 the parliamentarians ('Roundheads', with hair cut short) built 24 timber forts around London. The City pulpits and printing presses, with strong Puritan fervour, then exhorted Londoners to create a defensive bulwark against the royal forces. The response was immediate. *The Diurnal* (perhaps exaggerating) reports that after an Ordinance promulgated in the churches on 30 April 1643:

> on the following Wednesday many thousands of men and women (good housekeepers), their children and servants, went out of the several parishes of London with spades, shovels, pickaxes and baskets, and drums and colours before them, some of the chief men of every parish marching before them, and so went into the fields and worked hard all day in digging and making trenches from fort to fort … and late at night the company came back … and the next day many more went, and so they continued daily, with much cheerfulness[35].

One day 2,000 porters went 'in their white frocks', and on another five to six thousand tailors. The Common Council and the Trained Bands with 'many substantial citizens, their wives and families went to digge'[35]. For many days as many as 20,000 people, from every parish and every trade, men and women alike, were said to have marched out with their shovels to dig for victory. Many of Staple Inn's inhabitants must have felt the need to play their part, since the defences passed only a few hundred metres away.

By summer 1643 the 24 forts were linked by eighteen miles of defensive ditches and earth ramparts, some up to 18 feet high, round the suburbs of the City. They stretched, on both sides of the river, from Knightsbridge in the west to the Tower in the east, and from Shoreditch in the north to Newington in the south. For the first time the City and Westminster were united. (But not for long. In September

# STAPLE INN 1580–1700

Despite these troubles it seems that the Hall roof was rebuilt in 1655 – the head of a rainwater pipe shows that date.

The restoration of the monarchy in 1660 seemed to promise better times after the disappointments of the interregnum and the near anarchy in London in 1659 following Cromwell's death in 1658. Charles II brought an easy urbanity and cultural tone to a town long starved of that by the frigid pomp of his father and the military austerity of the interregnum. Among his initiatives he licensed new playhouses, the King's Theatre in Drury Lane and the Duke of York's in Lincoln's Inn Fields. For a few years hopes rose. The returning loyalists set up homes in the pleasant open spaces of Lincoln's Inn Fields, Covent Garden, Pall Mall, St James's and Soho Fields. The divide between 'Westenders' and the City's 'Eastenders' became more marked.

Meanwhile, however, the legal educational work of the Inns of Chancery had been struck a fatal blow by the political turmoil, never to recover. Worse was to follow.

## § 5.9 THE GREAT PLAGUE STRIKES STAPLE INN IN 1665

The dreaded plague had struck London regularly for hundreds of years. Bede (ca. 673–735) records the first epidemic in 664[54], although for several centuries leprosy was an even worse problem. In the 1530s a system of Bills of Mortality was introduced requiring each parish to submit weekly details of deaths and their cause. This gave early warning of plague epidemics, and also provided early data for the future life insurance industry. In 1563 17,500 Londoners died, about 20% of the population. More than 18,000 died in 1593, 30,000 in 1603 and 40,000 in 1625 when the life of the City came to a halt. The Bills of Mortality, which understated the situation, show St Andrew's Church, Holborn, burying 1,561 people in 1593, of whom 936 died from the plague, and 2,190 people in 1625, of whom 1,636 died from the plague[3].

After returning in 1636 and from 1638 to 1643, the plague came back with a flourish in 1665. Deaths in London totalled nearly 100,000. At its peak at least 6,000 people were buried every week. Plague pits for the dead were dug outside

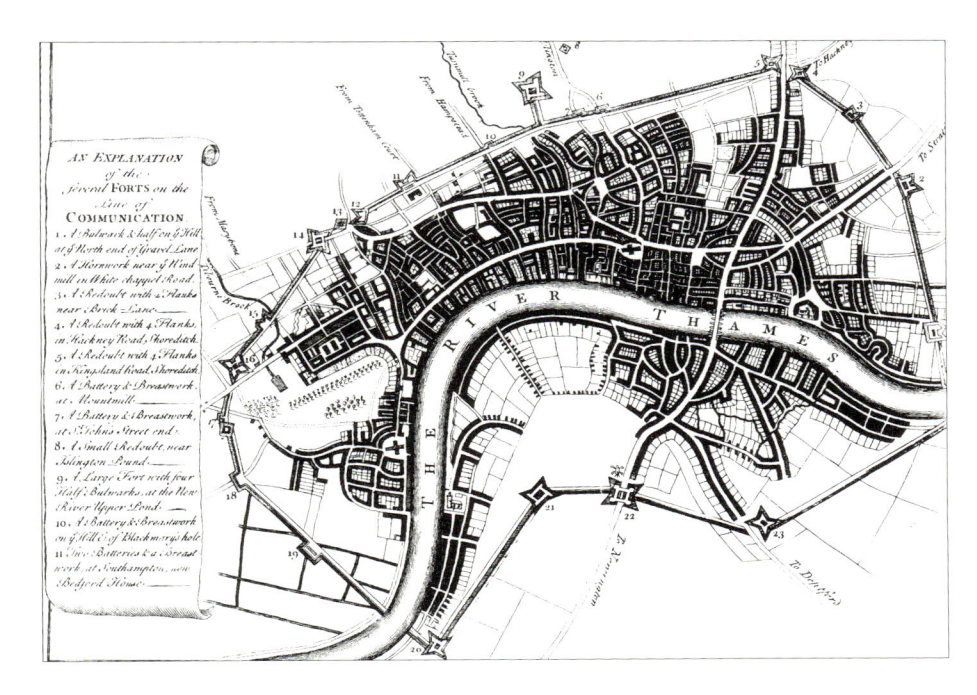

*London's fortifications against the Royalists 1642–1643. Fort 10 overlooks Gray's Inn Road.*
From W. Maitland, *The History of London from its foundation by the Romans to the present time, 1739.* (© Historical Publications Ltd)

1647 Parliament ordered all forts to be demolished.)

For the first time, too, Staple Inn was united with the City. One of the forts was a quarter mile away on Tot-hill near today's Mount Pleasant, commanding Gray's Inn road. The ramparts passed to the south of Guilford Street. Musketry and cannon-fire practice was heard regularly. Treasure was taken from the livery companies to finance Cromwell's New Model Army – the King finally losing largely through lack of money. Revolution was in the air, an uncomfortable feeling for many concerned with the maintenance of the law – and of a comfortable life-style.

# CHAPTER FIVE

the City walls, including pits in Holborn. The honeymoon period following the 1660 Restoration came to an abrupt end.

Few parishes escaped the plague in 1665, especially in the sprawling suburbs where the black rats had a field day among the sheds, stores, pigs and poultry. The epidemic started in St. Giles, the slum of slums, and spread quickly to Holborn, whose people were decimated. St Bartholomew's Hospital was swamped with patients. 3,958 parishioners of St Andrew's Church were buried, including 3,108 plague victims – on average nearly eleven buried every day throughout the year.

Samuel Pepys described in entries for 8 August and 4 September 1665 how the coachman driving him through Holborn:

> at last stood still, and came down hardly able to stand, and told me that he was suddenly struck very sick, and almost blind – he could not see... As to myself, I am very well, only in fear of the plague... And to Westminster Hall, where talking, hearing very sad stories. Poor Will, that used to sell us ale at the Hall door, his wife and three children died, all I think in a day. So home through the City again, wishing I may have taken no ill in going; but I will go I think no more thither.... but it troubled me to pass by Coome farme where about 21 people have died of the plague... and a watch is being kept there day and night to keep the people in, the plague making us cruel as dogs one to another[34].

Officially people were locked in their house for forty days after infection had ended.

The inhabitants of Staple Inn must have suffered greatly, some through contracting the disease and all through fear of it. The old entrance doors were found in later restoration work to have had the rough red cross painted on them to show there was plague within. No doubt the words were added – 'Lord, have mercy on us'.

*'The Plague in 1665'. At its peak in London 6,000 were buried every week. A pioneering study of the Bills of Mortality in London by John Graunt would be a forerunner of actuarial science developed by mathematical analysts and later by professional actuaries.*
(© Institute of Actuaries Library)

Some Staple Inn residents might have fled to live by or on the river, where the disease did not get a hold (10,000 people did just that) or to their country homes in the hope of escape, but their welcome might understandably have been less than enthusiastic. Work at Staple Inn declined dramatically that year, and at times stopped. The river and streets were largely deserted. A melancholy 'watcher' stood outside the affected doorways. Furtive pedestrians passed carefully 'on the other side', amid the creaking of the 'dead carts' on their way to the funeral pyres. Pepys wrote again on 20 September:

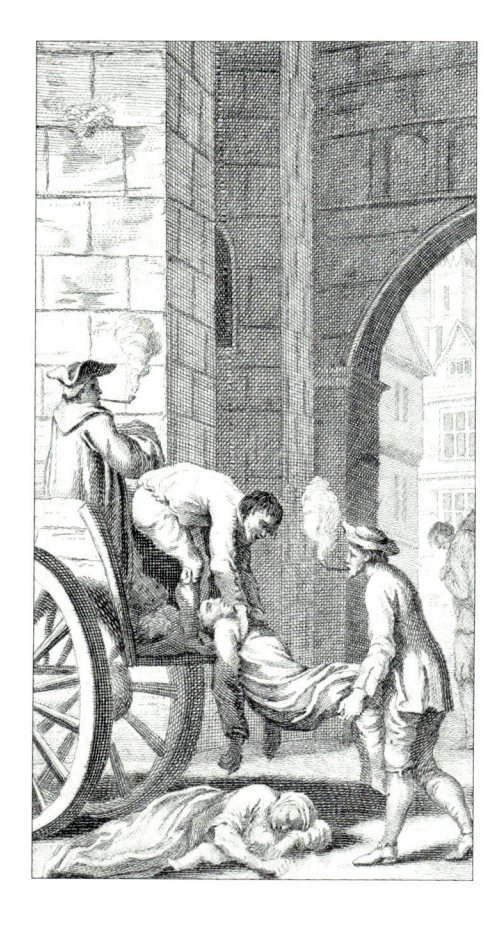

> But, Lord! What a sad time it is to see no boats upon the River; and grass grows all up and down White Hall court, and nobody but poor wretches in the streets![34]

As winter's cold returned the plague subsided, and by January 1666 people were returning to the City.

§ 5.10 THE 1666 GREAT FIRE MISSES STAPLE INN
AND LEAVES A 221-YEAR LEGACY

Eight months later the inhabitants of Staple Inn were more fortunate when two-thirds of the City was destroyed by the Great Fire of 1666. More than 13,000 houses, 44 livery halls, and 87 parish churches were burnt. The godly could be heard attributing the disasters of 1665 and 1666 to divine retribution for the evils of the Restoration, and Roman Catholics were also blamed for plotting the Great Fire.

Strong winds from the east fanned the fire from its start in Pudding Lane near London Bridge at 1.00 a.m. on Sunday 2 September. It reached Temple Church to the south and came near but not quite to St Andrew's Church and the Holborn Bridge. It crossed Gunpowder Alley near Fetter Lane. One of the nine recorded deaths in the fire was in Shoe Lane, 300 yards from Staple Inn, when Paul Lovell refused to leave his home and was burnt[29]. The diary of John Evelyn (1620–1706) records:

> I went on horseback and it was now gotten as far as Inner Temple, all Fleet Street, Old Bailey, Ludgate Hill, Warwick Lane, Newgate, Pauls Chain, Watling Street now flaming and most of it reduced to ashes, the stones of St. Paul's flew like grenades, the lead melting down the streets in a stream …[18]

On the Tuesday evening the wind died down, and by Wednesday the fire stopped half way up Fetter Lane, 200 yards from Staple Inn.

We do not know how Staple Inn coped at that time. Did the residents leave for the open fields to the north and west, as did most of the City's inhabitants? There were many thousand people in makeshift shelters on Moorfields less than a mile away in the days following the fire. On 5 September Pepys wrote:

> walked into Moorefields (our feet ready to burn, walking through the towne among the hot coles), and find that full of people, and poor wretches carrying their goods there…[34]

Did strangers fleeing from south and east stop in Staple Inn for shelter? How black and how illuminated were the skies, and how deep the ash on the ground? Pepys wrote on 2 and 4 September:

> We saw the fire as only one arch of fire from this to the other side of the bridge, and in a bow up the hill for an arch of above a mile long: it made me weep to see it. The houses all on fire and flaming at once; and a horrid noise the flames made, and the cracking of houses at their ruine. … Saw how horridly the sky looks, all on a fire in the night, was enough to put us out of our wits; and indeed it was extremely dreadful, for it looks just as if it was at us, and the whole heaven on fire[34].

Fortunately the fire stopped short of the large gunpowder store in the Tower of London, or indeed 'the whole heaven' would have seemed on fire.

On 7 September Evelyn wrote:

> I then went towards Islington and Highgate where one might have seen 200,000 people of all ranks and degrees, dispersed and laying along by their heaps of what they could save from the fire, deploring their loss and though ready to perish for hunger and destitution, yet not one asking one penny for relief, which appeared a stranger sight than any I had yet beheld[18].

The sturdy Pepys, who had left his home, was much affected by the disaster, writing on 7 and 8 September:

> I home late to Sir W. Pen's, who did give me a bed, but without curtains or hangings, all being down. So here I went the first time into a naked bed, only my drawers on… but still both sleeping and waking had a fear of fire in my heart, that I took little rest… I met with many people undone, and more that have extraordinary great losses[34].

# CHAPTER FIVE

*Map showing the extent of the Great Fire of 1666. Staple Inn narrowly escaped as the fire stopped 200 yards short at Fetter Lane. From W. Maitland, The History of London from its foundation by the Romans to the present time, 1739.  (© Institute of Actuaries Library)*

By 15 September he was still 'much terrified in the nights now-a-days with dreams of fire and falling down of houses'. Fifteen days after the fire started Pepys wrote:

> By water, seeing the City all the way, a sad sight indeed, much fire being still in. And thence by coach over the ruins down Fleete Streete and Cheapside to Broad Streete[34].

It must have seemed an apocalyptic nightmare to Staple Inn's residents, recently returned after the plague. And soon there were bills to pay, due to new building regulations urgently introduced for rebuilding the City. Staple Inn's timber frontage overlooking the road had to be covered with a fireproof layer of plaster. The projecting bay windows were removed to the Hall's cellars, and the windows set back in line with the walls, since projecting higher floors increased the risk of fire spreading from house to house in narrow streets. The Elizabethan exterior was not restored until 1887.

There was a vast expansion in brick making within a mile of Staple Inn at St Giles and Moorfields, and an invasion of labour from outside London to carry out the rebuilding. The busy flow of traffic and people along Holborn road changed dramatically from the empty streets of 1665.

*Cheapside welcoming Marie de Medici in 1638. All timbered houses were destroyed by the fire 28 years later, changing Staple Inn from one of many to a rare survivor.*

(© Historical Publications Ltd)

*Staple Inn front houses on Holborn in 1854 – the fireproof plaster covering was a 221-year legacy of the Great Fire of 1666 that Staple Inn had just escaped.*

Watercolour by T. C. Dibdin, 1854.   (© Institute of Actuaries)

One salutary change following the Fire was the virtual elimination of plague in London, for reasons that are not clear. The cleansing effects of the Fire may have helped, but St Giles, a major centre of the plague, was not burnt. Perhaps there were some improvements in quarantine, sanitary arrangements and rodent control, but its disappearance is something of a mystery.

Another change was the development of insurance against fire – 25,000 Londoners had it by 1710. One pioneer in fire insurance was Nicholas Barbon, a builder who developed land to the north of Holborn road, including Red Lion Square on a seventeen-acre paddock, in the 1670s and 1680s. Barbon was the son of 'Praise God Barebones', a rich leather merchant and notorious Puritan fanatic who lived in Fetter Lane and after whom Cromwell's 1653 Little Parliament was named. Nicholas showed in his *Discourse of Trade* of 1690 a fine sense of economic theory for his time, but his approach to building development was unscrupulous and aroused much local opposition. In 1684 a hundred Gray's Inn law students fought his workmen to try to stop building on their recreation fields. Both the official and the unofficial hands of the law were ineffective.

Also unsuccessful was the attempt to reopen the Fleet river to commercial shipping by creating a 50 feet wide canal for 700 metres to the Thames. New wharves and storehouses were built along its banks up to Holborn Bridge. Sadly the bad habits of earlier years returned, and the river was soon swamped with rubbish and sewage.

Although not destroyed by the fire, St Andrew's Church was in poor condition, and in 1689 the parishioners employed Christopher Wren to design a new building, much as it stands today. It is the largest of Wren's parish churches.

§ 5.11 THE SOCIETY OF STAPLE INN IN A SORRY STATE IN THE LATE SEVENTEENTH CENTURY

The last quarter of the seventeenth century was difficult for the Inns. The Civil War ruined many English country gentlemen who could no longer afford to send their sons to Inns of Chancery or of Court. The spread of printing made 'distance learning' much easier. Admissions fell away, and the old system of education was greatly reduced or lapsed. Only one student moved from Staple Inn to Gray's Inn between 1690 and 1746. The lifestyle had to be curtailed, and the tensions of living through unprecedented political, physical and emotional trauma, including at times strife within the Inns, must have taken a severe toll on many residents. The recovery and forward-looking approach of the next generation at Staple Inn is all the more remarkable for that.

Strong leadership from the Principals was needed. Confidence in Richard Kilburne (1605–1678) was clearly high since he was Principal through the troubles from 1664 and for five terms until his death. An eminent solicitor in chancery, a Justice of the Peace in Kent, and author of works on the topography of Kent, he was married with nine children. He and his immediate predecessors and successors, largely unknown now, must have included some strong, fine men.

CHAPTER SIX

# *Recovery and Transition from Law School to 'Club' in the Eighteenth Century*

## § 6.1 MAJOR REBUILDING AT STAPLE INN, 1729–1780

Staple Inn fared better than many Inns of Chancery, whose owners failed to manage their property and finances effectively through the difficult times. The vigorous nature of life at Staple Inn is well illustrated by the new building work funded by the Society in the eighteenth century, when virtually the whole complex was rebuilt except for the Holborn frontage and the Hall. No. 9 was rebuilt in 1729 and No. 7 in 1731 by Principal Robert Jenkyn, No. 8 in 1734 by Principal Thomas Warde, and No. 10, overlooking the south garden, in 1747 by Principal John Thompson. (See section 7.6 for reference to the 'mysterious' 'PJT' in Charles Dickens' *The Mystery of Edwin Drood*.) No. 8 has a lead rainwater head inscribed 'TPW 1734'. Thomas Leech replaced the north door from the courtyard into the Hall, and the south door of the Hall facing the garden in 1753 with the Georgian Gothic style we see today. The inscription:

T    L
P
17   53

over the door into the garden was perhaps in friendly competition with 'PJT' at No. 10.

The *Gentleman's Magazine* reported on 27 November 1756 that a fire had 'entirely consumed' No. 1 Staple Inn. The

*The south door in honour of Thomas Leech, Principal of Staple Inn from 1753.*

(Staple Inn Hall

© Prudential Corporation plc)

owners of the four chambers there 'and several others escaped with the utmost difficulty', but four people died. They were the sister in law of one of the chamber owners (she having 'arrived from the country' the previous night), two of his children and their nurse.

This tells us something about the use of a Staple Inn house at that time. If 'several' is taken to be only four, there were twelve people sleeping in the house that night, and it was clearly home for one or more families with close links with 'the country'.

No. 1 was rebuilt in 1757 (insured value £680 16s 6d, rebuilding cost £1,053), and the damaged No. 2 in 1759, both by Principal Thomas Leech. There is a record of the fire in stone over the entrance to No. 1 – '*Surrexit ex Flamis Anno. Don. 1757 Thoma. Leech Principali Iterumque reaedificata 1954*'. The latter reference is to the rebuilding after the 1944 flying bomb, with the same note over the doors of Nos. 3, 9 and 10. Sadly most of the Inn's archives were destroyed in the 1756 fire.

The clock in the Hall dates from before 1757. It is driven by two huge weights running in a channel in the wall. In 1757 two clock faces were added, one for the courtyard and one for the garden, all operated by the same mechanism.

The hands on the original clock had stuck on the figures 6 and 8, giving rise to the pecuniary implication in the verse:

CHAPTER SIX

*Staple Inn Hall – Looking towards the gallery two years before the 1884 sale.*
Watercolour by J. Crowther, 1882. (© Guildhall Library, Corporation of London)

# RECOVERY AND TRANSITION FROM LAW SCHOOL TO 'CLUB'

*The Ancients' ancient clock was stopped*
*Stopped by the hand of fate;*
*The figures stood (of course they would)*
*Stuck fast at six-and-eight.*

Six shillings and eight pence, half a mark, one-third of one pound sterling, was a common ingredient in legal charges, as well as a burial fee.

This scale of rebuilding compares dramatically with the failing fortunes of Barnard's Inn, which Charles Dickens records in the next century as 'the dingiest collection of shabby buildings ever squeezed together in a rank corner as a club for tom-cats'[14]. The contrast in the fortunes of the two daughter colleges of the same Inn of Court shows how their fate was very much in the hands of their own inhabitants, with minimal control or financial support from the superior college. Occasional ceremonial links remained between Staple Inn and Gray's Inn, but the two institutions led essentially separate lives.

In this period of rebuilding the Principals started to donate stained glass windows to the Hall to mark their terms of office.

## § 6.2 NEW STAINED GLASS 1747–1880 – BUT WHY NONE DURING 1618–1747?

Between 1618 and 1725 for certain, and with three possible exceptions until 1747, no new stained glass windows were added in the Hall. Why?

The Address by Institute of Actuaries President Archibald Day on 22 November 1887 to the Institute's first annual meeting in the Hall may give clues. First, he states that 'the panelling of the hall is of oak, from which the paint has now been very carefully removed'. Second, in a footnote he adds that 'in the halls of the Middle Temple and Gray's Inn these panels are filled with armorial bearings'. Third, he quotes 'M.G.G.' in the *Pall Mall Gazette* of 1 November 1886 stating that the adornments of the Hall had been removed by the departing Ancients of the Society of Staple Inn (see section 8.1). 'The twelve Caesars, and the inn's hatchment, have gone – indeed I was offered a couple of emperors and

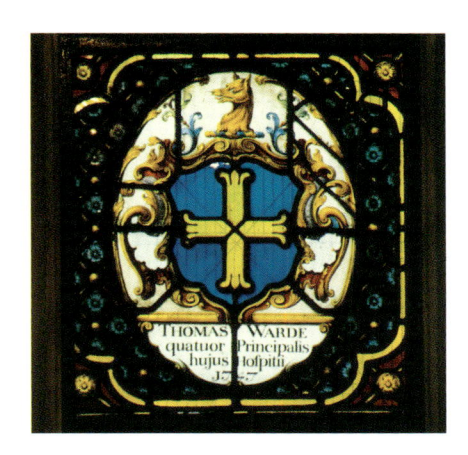

*With the woolsack 'insignia' of the Society of Staple Inn, the window of Thomas Warde set a tradition to mark the tenure in office of its Principals.*

(Staple Inn Hall © Prudential Corporation plc)

the woolpack for one pound, or three emperors at six-and-eight a head'. Finally, Day continues, 'The original charge for painting these arms on canvas, in the time of Charles II, was £10'[9].

It seems likely that from Reginald Knight, Principal in 1583, to Robert Jenkyn, Principal 1725–1734, the wall panels were used to record the Principals' terms in office, and were removed in 1884 when the Society was wound up, or in the 1887 restoration work (see section 8.5). There were about 35 Principals during this period. Perhaps the Principals before 1583 also followed the same practice.

This changed in 1747. Thomas Warde, Principal from 1734 to 1747, donated a panel in the top row of the oriel window, and set a pattern that was followed by every succeeding Principal except the last. There are 33 stained-glass windows of Principals from this period, the latest being that of Edward Walmisley, Principal from 1880 to 1884. His successor, Francis C. Domville Smythe, Principal when the Society was wound up and Staple Inn sold in 1884, does not have a stained glass panel.

## CHAPTER SIX

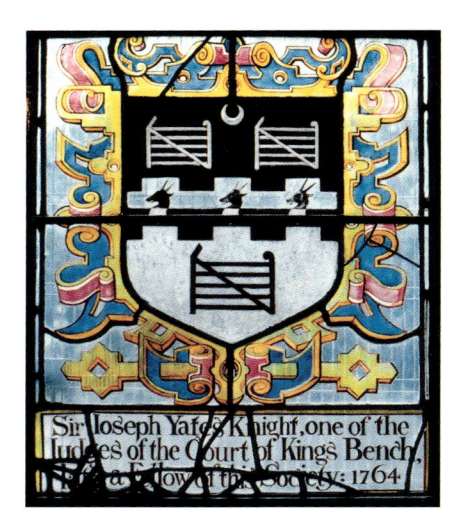

*The window for Sir Joseph Yates.*   *The window for Sir Alan Chambré*
(Staple Inn Hall © Prudential Corporation plc)

Two new panels were also added in 1764 and 1812, for Sir Joseph Yates and Sir Alan Chambré, immediately below the judges' panels from the 1612 to 1618 period. The windows mark their promotion to be Judges and Knights. The Chambré panel, bottom right, has exceptionally fine painted work, signed and dated James Pearson, 1812.

Most of the later eighteenth and nineteenth-century glass is less dramatic than the early windows installed soon after the Hall was built. The stained glass craft stopped under the Commonwealth in the mid-seventeenth century. When it resumed the available materials had changed to produce more insipid, although more delicate, draughtsmanship, requiring great skill in the use of paint, stain and enamels. The result is still wonderful, especially when the sun illuminates the colours and designs.

Sir Joseph Yates (1722–1770) from Lancashire was at Staple Inn from 1740 to 1748, before moving to Inner Temple, becoming a barrister there in 1753. He was employed by the Crown against John Wilkes in 1763, in which year he was knighted. Of high integrity, he stood up to the devious Chief Justice Lord Mansfield, resigning from the King's Bench to move to the junior Court of Common Pleas shortly before his death.

Sir Alan Chambré (1739–1823) came from Westmoreland in his late teens to work for a firm of solicitors in Pall Mall and joined the Society of Staple Inn in 1757 with the requisite dozen bottles of claret (see section 6.3). In 1758 he moved to Middle Temple and in 1764 to Gray's Inn where he became barrister in 1767 and Treasurer in 1783. He became a Serjeant-at-Law in a vacation period in 1799 following an untimely death. This required a special Act of Parliament since officially such appointments had to be made during term time. He was Justice of the Common Pleas from 1800 to 1815, and had a high reputation – 'among the most honest and amiable of men'.

Three windows of less certain date include the two on the left of the top row of the bay window, one of Queen Elizabeth I, the other of the insignia of Staple Inn. It is likely that Thomas Warde installed them with his panel in 1747. There is also one 'stray' window near the gallery, dated 1725 but almost certainly introduced later, in the name of Jonas Sedgly. He was admitted to Staple Inn in June that year. This window and its location on its own over the gallery are odd, since the shield is not a Sedgly coat, and it appears to be part of a window from elsewhere. The Principal in 1725 was Robert Jenkyn, whose name is inscribed over the doors of Nos. 7 and 9. It is unclear why his successor Thomas Warde decided to record his own long tenure as Principal in the more traditional stained glass manner as well as over the door of No. 8 – but it was a decision we may applaud.

The Hall was also adorned with paintings and sculptures. W. Herbert's low-key description of Staple Inn in 1804 refers to:

> a small garden, pleasantly laid out [and the Hall as a] modern erection … the interior forms a large handsome room, and is neatly kept… The hall contains some portraits, of no particular interest, and casts of the twelve Caesars, on brackets[24].

The portraits 'of no particular interest' were probably those of Charles II, Queen Anne, the Earl of Macclesfield, Lord Chancellor Cowper and Lord Camden, portraits which might have graced many a gentlemen's club of the day.

§ 6.3 STAPLE INN BECOMES 'PRACTICALLY A CLUB'
Earlier in the evolution of the legal system attorneys and the newer class of solicitors had to belong to an Inn, either of Court or of Chancery. In 1615 they were barred from the Inns of Court, which became the exclusive province of barristers. The Inns of Chancery had an opportunity, but they were unable to take it. Their teaching provision was grossly inadequate in quality and quantity for the developing needs of attorneys and solicitors. The last Gray's Inn Reader for Staple Inn was appointed in 1675. Better legal education developed around the country. A statute was passed in 1729 stating that attorneys were no longer required to belong to any Inn but should be trained through apprenticeship. Other organisations were formed in 1739 and 1825 from which the Law Society developed to serve the professional needs of attorneys and solicitors.

By 1730 there was work for 5,000 lawyers in London, but few practised from an Inn. Although in 1761 it was recorded that the Inns of Chancery were 'for the most part taken up by Attornies, Solicitors and Clerks', they were there for their chambers and residence. The training purpose of the Inns of Chancery had ended. They became little more than collections of residential chambers, or as E. Williams reports, 'practically a club'.[55]

This description was largely true for Staple Inn for most of the eighteenth century. There was a minor education flurry between 1746–1785 when twenty-three students moved to Gray's Inn. There was still a strong legal presence – in 1763 eighteen attorneys were listed as residing at Staple Inn – but the occupants were there for their own interests, not to promote the profession.

This was perhaps as well for them since the legal profession was not universally admired, indeed was popularly thought to be open to bribery. An 'ambidexter' was a lawyer who took fees from both plaintiff and defendant in the same case. The *London Chronicle* reported sourly of the Inns of Court (and by inference the Inns of Chancery) that:

> retirement here was intended to promote knowledge … but these seminaries are no longer possessed of their intended inhabitants. They are becoming lodging houses to the mean, the vicious, the ridiculous, the abandoned, to stockbrokers, gamesters… Their Dulcineas attend them with a long procession of fiddlers, cats, monkeys, French horns, dogs, pimps and parasites[36].

In contrast with the sad picture in the *London Chronicle*, the Society of Staple Inn actively maintained their Inn to good standards. For the freehold owners it was a financial investment. The courtyard was planted with flowers and shrubs. 'Commit no nuisance railings' were in place to deter ungentlemanly behaviour – two still serving their purpose by the Hall today. In the garden were flowers, shrubs and trees, including a fig tree spreading over nearly all the south side of the Hall. Children enjoyed these well-kept playgrounds, free from the dangers of passing horses and carriages, drunks, pickpockets and other undesirables in the busy streets outside. Staple Inn differed from other Inns, where a sharp contrast was reported between the clean and tidy private chambers and the scruffiness of the common areas.

The Society organised dinners regularly in Hall. The club character is illustrated by the entry fees and fines which were levied, for instance for dining guests of members, ('a bottle of red port wine' from 1757), and for new admissions and members on marriage ('twelve bottles of good clarett' from 1704 and 1717, with a fine of one gallon for daring to suggest a smaller entry fee). F. Fairbank was struck off in 1782 for not providing wine on his marriage[55]. Promotion to Ancient cost the lucky man one guinea from 1702.

§ 6.4 PRINCIPALS OF THE SOCIETY OF STAPLE INN, 1400–1884
E. Williams offers an order of the Principals of the Society of Staple Inn starting with Richard Champion, Principal 1580–1583[55], to which this book suggests only

minor variations. For the earlier period readers can consult recent findings from sixteenth- and seventeenth-century manuscripts by John Baker, who has traced records of sixteen Principals between 1456–1600. The panel for Nicholas Brocket, Principal in 1543, commemorates the earliest of those for whom stained glass evidence survives. The manuscripts also refer to coats of arms for Principals who followed Brocket but whose crests no longer survive in the Hall.

One assumption is that in the Society's early years most Principals were wool or other merchants, and that in time (mainly) lawyers took their place. They would all have been successful men, many with homes, estates and interests in the country to balance their life at the Inn.

Only two Principals are recorded in the *Dictionary of National Biography* – perhaps not surprising since an Inn of Chancery did not have the same status as an Inn of Court. After 1600 the Principals are unknown from about 1604 to 1620, from about 1626 to 1664, possibly from 1682 to 1688 (unless Samuel Ward served for three terms), and from 1694 to 1716. We therefore lack the names of many Principals, and have good career information about only two. Perhaps more research will bring others to life. The two who are recorded in the *Dictionary of National Biography* are Richard Kilburne (1605–1678) – (see section 5.11) – and Robert Kelham (1717–1808). Kelham, from Lincolnshire, was an attorney in King's Bench up to 1792, a distinguished antiquary, and writer of legal books. He was Principal from 1784 to 1787. His son Robert (1755–1811) was also an attorney in King's Bench but appears not to link with Staple Inn.

## § 6.5 SOME EIGHTEENTH- AND NINETEENTH-CENTURY RESIDENTS OF STAPLE INN

Members of the 'club' were long-term residents, others came and went. A land tax assessment for Staple Inn in 1799 lists 36 names as holding one or more sets of rooms in the twelve houses[58]. About 20% of the rooms had no named occupants.

An advertisement in *The Times* on 1 January 1785 implies there were 'genteel' families with children in the area:

*To let, small Lodgings Genteely Furnished, for a single Gentleman, in a house where there are no children. Enquire at No. 6, Staple Inn Buildings, Middle Row, Holborn.*

Isaac Reed (1742–1807), son of a Fleet Street baker, took chambers in No. 11 Staple Inn and became a member in 1769, after a brief spell in Gray's Inn. He established a good conveyancing practice, but his real passion was literary research and drama. He became a well-regarded editor of Shakespeare's works, and a generous host to numerous visitors and literary experts. Despite being diffident in public he was happy to be frank in private. He is said to be unique in not provoking the quarrelsome, cynical George Steevens (1736–1800). Steevens was a prolific commentator on Shakespeare who frequently visited Reed in Staple Inn, often late at night with a borrowed latch-key, to work on Shakespeare texts. Reed was President for many years of the 'Unincreasable Club', a gathering of people from many fields of art who met in the Queen's Head, Holborn. He collected a large, valuable library in Staple Inn. When he died, after long suffering, this was auctioned for £4,386 19s 6d, over 39 days.

John Murdoch (1747–1824) is an example of a man who was not a lawyer who lived in the Inn for many years from the 1780s. He taught French and English to students in their homes or in his rooms. Talleyrand, the French statesman, was one such pupil when he was living in exile in England for a period.

Richard Wordsworth (1768–1816), elder brother of William, had chambers in Staple Inn as an attorney early in the nineteenth century. John Robinson of Gray's Inn and Westmoreland left him a legacy when he died in 1802.

From January 1759 Dr Samuel Johnson (1709–1784), son of a Lichfield bookseller, was a tenant for a few months in the room over the entrance to No. 3. In 1748 he had lived in the Golden Anchor in Middle Row before moving to Gough Square where he lived for ten years and wrote his *Dictionary*. When he had completed this he could no longer afford the house in Gough Square – indeed he had been arrested in 1756 for a debt of £5 13s, for which he was fined £6 and released by a loan from a friend, Samuel Richardson. In Staple Inn

Johnson wrote *The History of Rasselas, Prince of Abyssinia*, a powerful assault on the fashionable optimism of the day, and his most popular work. Johnson likened this to Voltaire's *Candide*, hastily adding that they were written so closely one after the other that 'there was no time for imitation'[4]. The advance payment enabled him to pay the bills for his mother's funeral. Boswell reported that Johnson told Sir Joshua Reynolds that he composed it in the evenings of one week, sent it to the press in portions as it was written, and had never read it since. Later Boswell reported that, on a journey to Scotland in 1781:

> [Johnson] talked to us little in the carriage, being chiefly occupied in reading... his own 'Prince of Abyssinia', on which he seemed to be intensely fixed; having told us that he had not looked at it since it was first finished[4].

After a few months he moved to lodgings in Gray's Inn, and then to Inner Temple Lane. The great man was very short of money.

## § 6.6 SOCIAL DECLINE IN EIGHTEENTH-CENTURY HOLBORN

As Johnson's life illustrated (aided later by a Crown pension and Boswell's writings) London continued to provide endless stimulus and a wonderful quality of life for those who could access it, and Holborn shared in this. The Fleet river was arched over in 1733 from Holborn bridge to the Thames, and a market erected along the line of today's Farringdon Street. Thanks to the initiative of Sir Hans Sloane the British Museum opened in 1759, albeit only to a carefully vetted public. The surviving legal Inns were havens of intellectual and professional stimulus, (whatever the public perception of them). Less conventionally, Fetter Lane had since the 1650s been famous for its conventicles, meetings of religious dissenters. John Wesley preached in 1737 in the new Fetter Lane Independent Chapel, and Tom Paine (1737–1809) lived there for a time. Medicinal wells and spas near King's Cross became a major recreation area within reach of Staple Inn. The hallmarks on three fine pewter plates (held on indefinite loan by the Institute of Actuaries from the Prudential) suggest they were made by craftsmen

*Society of Staple Inn pewter dining plate of the late eighteenth century made near Staple Inn.*

(Archives of Prudential Corporation plc)

in and near Fetter Lane in the late eighteenth or early nineteenth century.

However, social decline in Holborn, which began in the seventeenth century, continued. In contrast with the stylish, cultured character of the early days of the legal invasion, the area became increasingly overcrowded and unhygienic, with a

# CHAPTER SIX

*'A North view of London' circa 1792. St Andrew's Church with its tower is right of centre.*

(© Archives of Prudential plc)

huge influx of labourers and unemployed. London's population expanded from 600,000 to one million during the century. Henry Fielding (1707–1754), novelist and magistrate, wrote in 1751:

> The following account I have had from Mr Welch, the High Constable of Holborn, that in the parish of St Giles's there are great numbers of houses set apart for the reception of idle persons and vagabonds… That as these places are thus adapted to whoredom so they are no less provided for drunkenness, gin being sold in them all at a penny a quartern… That in the execution of search warrants Mr Welch rarely finds less than twenty of these houses open for the receipt of all comers at the latest hours. That in one of these houses, and that not a large one, he hath numbered 58 persons of both sexes, the stench of whom was so intolerable that it compelled him in a very short time to quit the place. Among other mischiefs attending this wretched nuisance, the greater increase of thieves must necessarily be one[26].

London was gripped by an unprecedented wave of lawlessness in the first half of the eighteenth century. Organised gangs, thirty strong, enjoyed near immunity from arrest, due partly to lack of police. St Giles, Smithfield, Saffron Hill, White Friars were major crime centres. One gang, nearly a hundred strong, was proficient in 'every art of Cheating, Thieving and Robbing', had 'Officers and a Treasury', and 'rotten Members of the Law to forge a Defence for them, and a great number of False Witnesses ready to support it'[54].

Living conditions around Staple Inn deteriorated. Street fights were common and violent, crowds surrounding the combatants with shouts of 'a ring, a ring'. Wrestlers, sometimes females together, fought to exhaustion. Public whippings and executions were often the cause of special public holidays. The number of hangings in London totalled 281 between 1701 and 1750, 246 during the 1760s, and 501 in the 1780s. Many of these took place at Tyburn, after bumping their way along Holborn road by cart, hurdle, sledge – or landau.

In one respect walking on pavements became easier. The proliferation of signs hanging from buildings had become so troublesome that from 1762 they were banned, and signs had to be fastened to walls. House numbering started. However, the area around Staple Inn continued to suffer traffic blight owing in part to Middle Row and to the erratic behaviour of animals on their way to Smithfield. The nobility and gentry in the fashionable squares to the west caused the opening in 1756 of a new bypass ring road for drovers through open fields along the line of Marylebone, Euston and Pentonville Roads, 40 feet wide and unpaved. However a toll had to be paid. Flocks and herds continued to find short cuts through London, many passing near Staple Inn. A letter in the *Gentleman's Magazine* of May 1761 complains of the 'pernicious practice of driving cattle through the streets of this city'[36]. On one occasion a large ox driven by some 'fellows in a furious manner into Southampton Row… at one spring staked himself upon the iron railings next to the Duke of Bedford's wall' – and died.

Worst of all for most people was the continual threat of disease. The expectation of life in England in 1751 has been estimated for both men and women at 37 years. For Londoners it was much less, perhaps no more than about 25, partly due to very high infant mortality rates[36]. More than half London-born children died before age ten. Boys' average height at age thirteen was 4 feet 3 inches in the mid-eighteenth century compared with 5 feet in the mid-twentieth.

Thomas Coram's Foundling Hospital was established in Hatton Garden in 1743, and soon moved to splendid purpose-built premises in the fields north of Gray's Inn. It provided basic care and vocational training for babies and young children whose mothers could not cope. The demand is illustrated by 15,000 admissions (compulsory in return for state subsidy) in 45 months in 1756 to 1760, far too large a number for proper care. In 1760 it reverted to private charity status with many fewer entries, perhaps 200 a year. Part of the site is now Coram's Fields, where no adult is allowed unless accompanied by a child. Handel helped the hospital's early development with performances of *The Messiah* in the chapel, packed with 1,000 people, each year from 1750 until his death in 1759. Perhaps inspired by this, London's first permanent dispensary for relief of the infant poor was set up in Red Lion Square in 1769.

## CHAPTER SIX

Between 1720 and 1750 gin was priced very competitively relative to beer and other drink, and was a major killer. In St Giles, twenty minutes' walk from Staple Inn, one shop in four was a 'brandy-shop' (compared with one in fifteen in the City). In 1737 in London there were 8,659 brandy-shops and 'only' 6,000 ale houses. 9,000 children died through drinking gin in 1751. Dr Johnson declared that no man could be happy in the present conditions if he were not drunk, which perhaps illuminated another of his comments that 'there is nothing which has yet been contrived by man, by which so much happiness is produced as by a good tavern or inn'[29]. William Hogarth's influence – see his prints 'Gin Lane', set in St Giles, and 'Beer Street', disparaging gin against relatively innocuous beer – led to the 1751 Gin Act. National gin consumption reduced from 11 million gallons in 1751 to 7.5 million in 1752 and 3.6 million gallons in 1768[36,54].

At fifteen minutes' walk in the other direction from Staple Inn, Fleet prison provided the eighteenth-century equivalent of Gretna Green and especially Las Vegas for those wanting quick, private, cheap weddings. Fleet was the main prison for debtors, whose numbers were so large that many were allowed to live in the surrounding area, called the Rules or Liberties of the Fleet. Among the prisoners were clergymen who could not pay their debts, and who welcomed the opportunity to earn a bit on the side by offering cut-price weddings. Others cashed in. 'T.C.', a watchmaker, wore smart minister's dress 'personating a clergyman'. Fleet Street had many signs inviting customers to walk in and be married, J.C. Jefferson identifying about 40 keepers of 'marrying houses' in the area. John Malcolm reports in *Londinium Redivivum* that there were almost 3,000 marriages in the four months to 12 February 1705. In the 1740s more than half the weddings in London took place there. People came from far and wide. A gardener from Nîmes married a girl from Guernsey; Chelsea pensioners wed there to benefit from the charms of their new brides and from the fee they earned from the brides' parishes for taking the ladies off the poor law books; a Rotherhithe landlord reported that 'it was a common thing when a fleet comes in to have two or three hundred marriages in a week's time among the sailors'[36]. A clergyman who operated a rival service in Mayfair was fined and, unable to

*William Hogarth's 'Gin Lane' of 1751 in St. Giles.*
(© Historical Publications Ltd)

pay, was sent to the Fleet debtor's prison – where his business expanded. The fun ended when a 1754 Act tightened the wedding regulations to end this free and easy approach and the business moved to Gretna Green.

Also readily available were opportunities for sex. Even Casanova (1725–1798) was impressed with the London sex scene.

> I visited the bagnios where a rich man can sup, bathe and sleep with a fashionable courtesan, of which there are many in London. It makes a magnificent debauch and costs only six guineas.[36]

Was the Turk's Head bagnio in Chancery Lane such a 'respectable' establishment, or was it more in line with the disorderly brothels which proliferated in London, many within 20 minutes' walk of Staple Inn? Consult Harris's *List of Covent Garden Ladies or Man of Pleasure's Kalendar* which was sold in London bookshops for 2s 6d.[36]

§ 6.7 THE GORDON RIOTS, 1780

Social unrest took various forms. A notorious example was the rioting against pro-Roman Catholic legislation in 1780. A 50,000 strong march and petition to Parliament led by the fanatical Lord Gordon got out of control. Violent 'No Popery' and anti-Irish riots followed in various parts of London. Several prisons, including Fleet and Newgate, were burned and their occupants released. Even nearer to Staple Inn, the house of Lord Chief Justice Cox in Red Lion Square and the Black Swan gin distillery off Fetter Lane were wrecked. The pretext for the latter was the Roman Catholic religion of the distiller, Langdale, but the real target was the liquor. In their excitement the crowd set fire to the spirits, which spread along the roadway and destroyed the distillery, part of Barnard's Inn, and about 20 houses. Dr Warner, who was living in Barnard's Inn, said the next morning – 'There can be no living here even if the fire stops immediately. The whole place is a wreck'.

Charles Dickens, in *Barnaby Rudge*, gives a vivid account of the crowd's intoxication, in which many became human torches and died as they fell in the road:

> From the burning cellars, where they drank out of hats, pails, buckets, tubs and shoes, some men were drawn alive, but all alight from head to foot; who, in their unendurable anguish and suffering, making for anything that had the look of water, rolled, hissing, in this hideous lake, and splashed up liquid fire …[12]

Staple Inn narrowly escaped the wrath and madness of the crowd, but did not escape the aftermath. St Andrew's was affected more severely than any other parish in London. Many residential properties were required to contribute to the cost of the damage to Langdale and others. The bill for Staple Inn was £17, a significant sum, although less than the £30 charge on the damaged Barnard's Inn[58].

More than 450 people were killed or wounded in the riots. It was, as Dr Johnson[4] said, 'a time of terror'. Social unrest continued to find violent expression. France declared war on England in 1793, and the London authorities, fearing that the French revolutionary fervour would spread, took conscription powers. Popular objections to this included mob violence in Shoe Lane.

CHAPTER SEVEN

# *Nineteenth-century Staple Inn until 1884 – Ever more a 'Little Nook'*

For much of the nineteenth century developments around Staple Inn influenced its future course more than those inside. The 'club' continued its steady, professional existence, but dramatic changes were occurring outside, on the whole for the worse for 'club' members.

### § 7.1 CONDITION OF LONDON AROUND NINETEENTH-CENTURY STAPLE INN

London's population expanded from 1,096,784 in 1801 to 2,651,939 in 1851 and to 6,506,889 in 1901. The birth rate among London's permanent residents continued, as it had for centuries, to fall below the death rate. The huge population growth came through migration from the countryside and from abroad. In 1820 St Andrew's, Holborn held 456 weddings, 746 burials and, untypically, 1552 baptisms (many perhaps of recent immigrants?) – on average 7.5 events every day. In 1851 38% of London's population were recent migrants from abroad, including 109,000 from Ireland forced to move by severe famine at home.

William Wordsworth (1770–1850) came to town several times, and found a 'monstrous anthill on the plain'. He was amazed by the variety of life:

> the quick dance of colours, lights, and forms; the deafening din; the comers and goers face to face…the string of dazzling wares, shop after shop, with symbols, blazoned names …[29]

And of London's largest fair, Bartholomew Fair at Smithfield, he wrote:

> What a shock for eyes and ears! What anarchy and din, barbarian and infernal – a phantasma, monstrous in colour, motion, shape, sight, sound …[29]

This was fifteen minutes' walk from Staple Inn, which William probably visited when staying in London, to see his eldest brother, Richard, in chambers there as an attorney.

Part of the colour, motion, shape, sight and sound was of the highest quality, for instance of music, art and theatre. The British Museum had been rebuilt and opened to the 'vulgar class' in the 1820s, such that by 1848 it was characterised as 'a truly equalising place'.[29] The Royal Academy and other leading cultural centres of excellence were thriving. As Dr. Johnson had earlier said to Boswell, who enjoyed walking round Holborn – Boswell Street is near Red Lion Square – London offered 'all that life can afford'[36]. Ned Ward found 'the streets a living theatre'[29].

Part, however, was driven by man's baser instincts, with, by today's standards, outrageous behaviour and 'entertainment'. Although Clerkenwell, a few hundred metres away, became a great centre for makers of watches and other precision instruments, and of jewellery, gold and silver objects, and had pleasure and tea gardens, it also attracted large numbers of the poor and unruly, including many Irish immigrants. In 1848 a crowd of 60,000 'marched' from that area to the City and to the West End to vent their frustrations, fighting battles with the police. Farringdon Road, built in 1845–1846, and Clerkenwell Road (1878) passed through an infamous maze of slums, including the elegantly and no doubt accurately named Liquorpond Street.

Local shopping for fruit and vegetables, including famously cress, was improved by the opening in 1826 of Farringdon Market when Fleet Market was cleared for the construction of Farringdon Street. That there was still extreme poverty was exemplified by watercress girls, some as young as seven in thin cotton dresses and threadbare shawls, haggling with saleswomen before dawn,

# NINETEENTH-CENTURY STAPLE INN UNTIL 1884

*Smithfield Market – then the largest animal market in the world 500 metres from Staple Inn.*
(© Guildhall Library, Corporation of London)

washing and bundling the leaves at the pump, and roaming the streets crying 'water-creases, four bunches a penny, water-creases'. 5d represented good takings for a long day[54].

More significantly for life at Staple Inn the largest animal market in the world was 500 metres away at Smithfield. In 1846 210,000 sheep and 1,518,000 cattle were bought and sold, and many slaughtered there. The road outside Staple Inn must have been disturbed hugely by passing animals, despite the existence of the bypass further north. Live cattle were still driven and stampeded through the streets, even through Sunday congregations, and slaughtered in the market where the facilities were grossly inadequate. In *Oliver Twist* (1837–1838) Dickens records that:

> the ground was covered, nearly ankle-deep, with filth and mire; a thick steam perpetually rising from the reeking bodies of the cattle…the unwashed, unshaven, squalid and dirty figures constantly running to and fro, and bursting in and out of the throng, rendering it a stunning and bewildering scene, which quite confounded the senses[11].

Respite came in 1855 when the Market was closed. It reopened in new style in 1868 as the London Central Meat Market, with underground railway connection to the main railway stations.

In 1827 a young surgeon, William Marsden, found a young woman dying on the steps of St Andrew's Church. Unable to gain admission for her to any hospital without financial underwriting, he founded a hospital in 1828 with members of the Cordwainers Company, requiring no payment by patients. Their first meeting was in the Gray's Inn Coffee House. The Hospital started in Hatton Garden, and was named The Royal Free Hospital in 1837 at the request of its patron, Queen Victoria. It moved in 1843 to Gray's Inn road, and in 1974 to Hampstead. In April 1843 the first general hospital for women was founded in Red Lion Square, and moved to Soho Square in 1852. Expectation of life nationally had not increased much from a century earlier[3], up from about 37 to 40–42[42], and in London from perhaps about 25 to about 30.

National and London leaders lacked the experience and imagination to manage effectively the scale of change caused by the population explosion. In 1801 the physician to the London Public Dispensary identified five areas as especially notorious for their wretchedness. Three were near Staple Inn, to the east, north and west – Smithfield, Gray's Inn road to Bunhill Fields, and St Giles[29]. Cholera came to London for the first time in 1832, with major repeat visits in 1848, 1849 and 1854. Even more deaths were caused by tuberculosis, typhus and influenza. The state of health in Holborn at this time has been characterised as 'a permanent fever'. Average house occupancy in Holborn rose from 8.4 in 1841 to 10 in 1881. There was grossly inadequate space in churchyards for burials, despite the opening of major cemeteries in the countryside around London between 1832 to 1841. In 1859 George Godwin wrote about the 'Town Swamps in Clerkenwell and Holborn'[29]. Charles Dickens saw these back streets as among the worst in London – Oliver Twist was introduced to Fagin and his gang of boy thieves in Field Lane, Saffron Hill, next to Hatton Garden. The Clerkenwell workhouse was built for 150 inmates, but held 320. Survival was the order of the day, and difficult – forget the workhouse ideal of providing some basic education and work. And when death came for the very poor, a pauper's grave awaited them. There was an open 'poors' hole in the churchyard of St Giles – 'how noisome the stench is …'[36] – and just a short walk from Staple Inn.

Reasons for the high death rate included overcrowding, malnutrition, infectious diseases, atmospheric pollution, poor drinking water, and the state of sanitation.

## § 7.2 SANITATION IN NINETEENTH-CENTURY LONDON

Early nineteenth-century London could be described as a City standing on an underground cavern of excavated cesspits. Most houses, presumably including Staple Inn, had cesspits under their floors. There were, however, only an inadequate 15 miles of sewers in all London to take the waste away – and those mainly in the more prosperous areas. In theory householders removed their cesspit contents to public laystalls, which were cleared by night cart men, or if you were well off they came to your house. However practice was far from perfect. By the middle of the century sewage backup from cesspits was commonly causing overflows to rooms above, and sometimes as 'friendly gifts' to neighbours. The stench was ever-present, since, although the U-bend had been invented by an ingenious watchmaker in 1775, many decades passed before its benefits were spread widely through the town. The growth in population presented problems that no government had faced before, and the response was woefully inadequate. Street-gulleys and streams became ever more choked and unpleasant, with nowhere to go except the Thames. This became a huge open sewer, recycling with each tide, 'as much liquid biology as liquid history', as Stephen Inwood characterises it[29].

Climax of a kind came with the 'Great Stink' in the hot, dry summer of 1858. It persisted on and off for ten years. Staple Inn was well within range. At last the politicians agreed to tackle London's sewerage system seriously. Based on contour maps specially prepared for the project (part of the Ordnance Survey) five huge brick tunnels, 82 miles long, were built on both sides of the Thames by 1875, connecting with 1,300 miles of sewers, on three levels. This marvellous engineering construction, linked with drainage schemes including the Albert, Victoria and Chelsea Embankments, dramatically improved sewerage and drainage. Cholera epidemics ceased. The schemes still serve London well. [At the time of writing, Thames Water offer a splendid walk through an underground section at Beckton – well worth a visit, not that daunting, and good for dinner table stories afterwards.]

The drainage and sewerage system provided a splendid promenade along the banks of the Thames, and reduced one form of 'Great Stink'. It did not, however, abate the growing menace of the London 'pea-soup' fogs, caused by vast quantities of coal burning for warmth and cooking. The opening chapter of Dickens' *Bleak House* (1853) paints a typically powerful picture of the horror of the 'London particular' fog:

> Fog everywhere. Fog up the river…; fog down the river … Fog on the Essex marshes, fog on the Kentish heights… Fog in the eyes and throats of ancient Greenwich pensioners… fog in the… pipe of the wrathful skipper…; fog cruelly pinching the toes of the shivering little boy on deck [13].

A music hall song brings in the girls as well – 'I'm just a little girl lost in the fog, me and my dog. Won't some kind gentleman see me 'ome?'

If Staple Inn's residents could to some extent shut themselves off from the horrors outside, they could not escape the 'Great Stink', nor the interminable fogs. To many with the possibility of escape to the countryside that option

*The London Particular Fog in 1872.*
William Small in *The Graphic* of 9 November 1872.
(© Mary Evans Picture Library)

became increasingly attractive. As the contemporary accounts below suggest, the contrast between Staple Inn and its surroundings, and between life in the Staple Inn area and life in the countryside outside London, was becoming ever more marked.

§ 7.3 AN AMERICAN VIEW OF STAPLE INN IN 1855: 'THAT LITTLE ISLAND OF QUIET'

Nathaniel Hawthorne (1804–1864) painted the contrast between Staple Inn and its surroundings in his *Passages from the English Notebooks* of 1855 when he was United States Consul in Liverpool:

> In Holborn I went through an arched entrance, over which was 'Staples Inn', and here likewise seemed to be offices; but in a court opening inwards from this, there was a surrounding seclusion of quiet dwelling houses, with beautiful green shrubbery and grass plots in the court, and a great many sunflowers in full bloom. The windows were open; it was a lovely summer afternoon, and I had a sense that bees were humming in the court, though this may have been suggested by my fancy, because the sound would have been so well suited to the scene. A boy was reading at one of the windows. There was not a quieter spot in England than this, and it was very strange to have drifted into it so suddenly out of the bustle and rumble of Holborn; and to lose all this repose as suddenly as on passing through the arch of the outer court. In all the hundreds of years since London was built, it has not been able to sweep its roaring tide over that little island of quiet[23].

§ 7.4 ANTHONY TROLLOPE'S OBSERVATIONS ON 'QUIET, DINGY NOOKS' IN 1864

In *Can You Forgive Her?* Anthony Trollope (1815–1882) takes the reader on a mystery tour, suggesting that Staple Inn had become a backwater:

> Opening off from Chancery Lane are various other small lanes, quiet, dingy nooks, some of them in the guise of streets going no whither, some being thoroughfares to other dingy streets beyond, in which sponging-houses abound, and others existing as the entrances to so-called Inns of Court – inns of which all knowledge has for years been lost to the outer world of the laity, and, as I believe, lost almost equally to the inner world of the legal profession. Who has ever heard of Symonds' Inn? … Of Staples' Inn, who knows the purposes or use? Who are its members, and what do they do as such? And Staples' Inn is an inn with pretensions, having a chapel of its own, or, at any rate, a building which, in its external dimensions, is ecclesiastical, having a garden and architectural proportions; and a façade towards Holborn, somewhat dingy, but respectable, with an old gateway, and with a decided character of its own[52].

The 'somewhat dingy but respectable' façade was the plaster placed over the original Elizabethan front after the 1666 Great Fire.

§ 7.5 DEMOLITION OF MIDDLE ROW, 1867

Less mysterious was Middle Row that dominated the street by the junction with Gray's Inn road for about 400 years. Perhaps initially smaller, it was developed to five storeys high. An 1838 plan of Middle Row shows 17 houses[37], including two Public Houses, and an 1865 plan shows 16 houses, including a Public House and a wine vault[17]. On busy days it and its business seriously checked the flow of traffic along Holborn road. Its 25 to 50 feet width restricted the roadway for traffic to as little as 35 feet. There were numerous complaints about this over many years, including one in 1657 describing it as:

> a mighty hindrance to Holborn in point of prospect, which if they were taken down there would be from Holborn Conduit to St Giles in the Fields one of the fairest rising streets in the world[37].

# NINETEENTH-CENTURY STAPLE INN UNTIL 1884

*The demolition of Middle Row in late 1867 would bring Staple Inn into the light.*
From Illustrated London News of 28 September 1867.   (© Archives of Prudential plc)

Proposals for removing Middle Row, requiring an Act of Parliament, were put to the Select Committee on Metropolis Improvements in 1836 and 1838. No action was taken. The Holborn District Board took up the proposal with the Metropolis Board again in 1856, with a scheme at net estimated cost of £46,625 to overcome the 'inconvenience, unsightliness and obstruction to traffic'[37]. The proposal was agreed, but fell foul of the linked plan to buy the freehold of Staple Inn and the buildings facing Middle Row to 'improve' the frontage which would be made more visible by its removal. These negotiations, perhaps not surprisingly, proved difficult.

The Holborn District Board tried again, unsuccessfully, in 1860, and in 1862 brought a modified proposal to remove the houses on the north side of Middle Row. The Metropolis Board agreed this was desirable, but decided it had too low priority to justify action.

In May and October 1865 the Holborn District Board tried yet again, aided this time by a deputation of local inhabitants, including surely some from Staple Inn. They pointed out that the Corporation of London had just approved the construction of Holborn Viaduct, and that this would cause enormous increase in traffic along Holborn road. The proposed demolition scheme was approved, at estimated cost £61,152, together with the decision not to purchase the buildings to the south of Middle Row. That 'would not be expedient, nor a financial gain'[37], and there were doubts about destroying one of the most picturesque examples of half-timber and plaster building. The Whitehall and Holborn Improvement Act was passed in 1865, and the demolition completed, at a cost of £76,415, in time for the road to be reopened to the public in December 1867. The minimum width of the road increased from 35 to 80 feet. The Staple Inn frontage was preserved, and was no longer 'overshadowed'.

The *Illustrated London News* celebrated with a full-page picture and article on 28 September 1867:

> The unsightly and inconvenient block of buildings, mostly in a very indifferent state of repair, which have hitherto obstructed the great thoroughfare of Holborn… are now being removed… After the removal of the archways and gates, the site of Holborn Bars was still commemorated by a pair of granite obelisks, at which not many years ago all carts and carriages not belonging to City freemen were obliged to stop and pay toll, the yearly amount of these tolls being £5,000. In the Golden Anchor, a house of Middle Row, Dr Johnson had a lodging in 1740. Below the Bars, on the right-hand side going down Holborn-hill, are several ancient and picturesque houses with the gable-ends of their roofs towards the street which the rage of modern innovation will perhaps spare a little longer, as they are not in the way of public traffic. As for the loss of Middle Row it is no matter for regret.

### § 7.6 CHARLES DICKENS AND STAPLE INN AS 'A LITTLE NOOK', 1853 AND 1870

Charles Dickens (1812–1870) knew Holborn well through living and working in the area, including five years in Furnival's Inn from 1834 to 1839, where he wrote The Pickwick Papers. He offered a glimpse of Staple Inn in *Bleak House* of 1853:

> Mr Snagsby being in his way rather a meditative and poetical man loved to walk in Staple Inn in the summertime and to observe how countrified the sparrows and the leaves are[10].

His final novel *The Mystery of Edwin Drood*, half-finished in 1870, was less flattering, suggesting a mysterious run-down backwater which cannot escape the fog, clash and gloom of London around it[15], compared unfavourably with the cloistered calm of Rochester ('Cloisterham'). Both, however, compare favourably with East End opium dens reeking of evil and corruption which also feature in chapter 11 of the unsolved murder story:

> Behind the most ancient part of Holborn where certain gabled houses some centuries of age still stand looking on the public way, as if disconsolately looking for the Old Bourne that has long run dry, is a

little nook composed of two irregular quadrangles called Staple Inn. It is one of those nooks, the turning into which, out of the clashing street, imparts to the relieved pedestrian the sensation of having put cotton in his ears, and velvet soles on his boots. It is one of those nooks where a few smoky sparrows twitter on smoky trees, as though they called to one another, 'Let us play at country', and where a few feet of garden-mould and a few yards of gravel enable them to do that refreshing violence to their tiny understandings. Moreover, it is one of those nooks which are legal nooks; and it contains a little Hall, with a little lantern in its roof: to what obstructive purposes devoted, and at whose expense, this history knoweth not.

In the days when Cloisterham took offence at the existence of a railroad afar off, as menacing that sensitive constitution, the property of us Britons: the odd fortune of which sacred institution it is to be in exactly equal degrees croaked about, trembled for, and boasted of, whatever happens to anything, anywhere in the world: in those days no neighbouring architecture of lofty proportions had arisen to overshadow Staple Inn. The westering sun bestowed bright glances on it, and the south-west wind blew into it unimpeded.

Neither wind nor sun, however, favoured Staple Inn one December afternoon towards six o'clock, when it was filled with fog, and candles shed murky and blurred rays through the windows of all its then-occupied sets of chambers; notably from a set of chambers in a corner house in the little inner quadrangle, presenting in black and white over its ugly portal the mysterious inscription:

P
J T
1747

In which set of chambers, never having troubled his head about the inscription, unless to bethink himself at odd times on glancing up at it, that haply it might mean Perhaps John Thomas, or Perhaps Joe Tyler, sat Mr Grewgious writing by his fire[15].

At that time Rochester (near where Dickens died) was connected to the London railway by omnibus. The 'neighbouring architecture', Middle Row, had been demolished three years earlier in 1867 (see section 7.5). JPT was Principal John Thompson who rebuilt No. 10 in 1747.

In chapter XVII of *Edwin Drood*, Reverend Septimus Crisparkle visited the prime suspect as the possible murderer of the mysteriously vanished Drood, in Staple Inn. Mr Grewgious had installed the suspect there as a 'law student'.

Full many a creaking stair he climbed before he reached some attic rooms in a corner, turned the latch of their unbolted door, and stood beside the table of Neville Landless. An air of retreat and solitude hung about the rooms and about their inhabitant. He was much worn and so were they. Their sloping ceilings, cumbrous rusty locks and grates, and heavy wooden bins and beams slowly mouldering withal, had a prisonous look, and he had the haggard face of a prisoner. Yet the sunlight shone in at the ugly garret window, which had a pent-house to itself thrust out among the tiles; and on the cracked and smoke-blackened parapet beyond, some of the deluded sparrows of the place rheumatically hopped, like little feathered cripples who had left their crutches in their nests; and there was a play of living leaves at hand that changed the air, and made an imperfect sort of music in it that would have been melody in the country[15].

## § 7.7 COMMUTER TRANSPORT IMPROVES IN THE SECOND HALF OF THE NINETEENTH CENTURY

For long journeys turnpike roads with good surfaces had started to appear late in the eighteenth century. The length of travel is illustrated by the official stagecoach timetable in 1790 which quotes 11 hours for London to Dover (71 miles), 6 hours for Dover to Calais (21 miles), and 50 hours plus stops for London to Paris (315 miles). However improvements were on the way. By 1845 the omnibus, an elongated coach seating about twenty passengers and pulled by three horses, replaced the slower, less reliable and more expensive short stagecoach, offering better travel between London and its suburbs. (According to Dickens' *Sketches by Boz* of 1836 they had also mastered the practice of a second bus keeping constantly behind the first one[10].) For local journeys the more efficient cabriolet (cab), with two or three seats and one horse, put the hackney carriages out of business by 1850, when there were 4,000 cabs in London.

The opening of New Oxford Street in 1845 to connect Oxford Street with Holborn, cutting through a maze of streets and St Giles slums, made traffic congestion in Holborn awful, relieved to some extent by the removal of Middle Row in 1867 and the 1869 opening of Holborn Viaduct, (its construction having cleared away more slums).

Escape to the countryside was becoming more practical. Dickens' 'railroads afar off' were accessible from Staple Inn. Euston Station opened as early as 1837, Waterloo in 1848, King's Cross in 1852, Victoria Station in 1860. The first line direct from Holborn Viaduct station to the south bank opened in 1864. The world's first underground train route opened in 1863 from Paddington to Farringdon, near Staple Inn, carrying nearly ten million passengers in its first year. The Circle Line was completed in 1884, serving most main line stations – with some discomfort. These early underground lines used steam engines, causing smoky, uncomfortable travel.

Big improvement came with the Central underground line from Bank to Shepherd's Bush which opened in 1900, with electric lifts. This 'Twopenny Tube' was the first 'modern' electric line – clean, cheap and fast, carrying 41 million passengers in 1901 – and of great benefit to Staple Inn. A motorbus service started in 1897, and electric tramcars in 1900, both big improvements on the horse-drawn versions. By then there were 250,000 horses in London, each producing annually three to four tons of dung.

Home-to-work travel between Staple Inn and the countryside was becoming much easier and more pleasant by late in the nineteenth century.

*Building Holborn Viaduct in the late 1860s – St Andrew's Church is seen top left.*
(© Guildhall Library, Corporation of London)

§ 7.8 THOMAS CARLYLE: LONDON – A PLACE TO VISIT RATHER THAN LIVE

After moving from Scotland to Chelsea in 1834 Carlyle wrote to his family:

> Of this enormous Babel of a place I can give you no account in writing: it is like the heart of all the universe; and the flood of human effort rolls out of it and into it with a violence that almost appals one's very sense… O that our father saw Holborn in a fog! … With the black vapour brooding over it, absolutely like fluid ink; and coaches and wains and sheep and oxen and wild people rushing on with bellowings and shrieks thundering din… It is a monstrous Wen…

# NINETEENTH-CENTURY STAPLE INN UNTIL 1884

*A million of vehicles, from the dog or donkey-barrow to the giant wagon, grind along its streets forever… There is an excitement in all this, which is pleasant as a transitory feeling, but much against my taste as a permanent one. I had much rather visit London than live in it[26].*

Fifty years later, with a further doubling of London's population, the minds of many professional people, including those in Staple Inn, were inclining towards Carlyle's view that it was becoming a place to visit for work rather than a place in which to live.

## § 7.9 THE SOCIETY OF STAPLE INN – WORTH MORE DEAD THAN ALIVE?

In 1811 the Society acquired the freehold of Staple Inn for £16,000 from the Gray's Inn Ancients who had owned it formally, but without charging rent, since 1529[55]. William Townsend of Hitchin was in the twenty-fourth of his twenty-seven years as Principal – which may suggest no great competition for the post. (Looked after by his sister, he asked in his will that she should be allowed to continue to reside there at a moderate rental – so perhaps space was not at a premium.) The new mace acquired in 1816 may perhaps be seen as a symbol of the new independence. In 1826 the rear elevation of the buildings on the street was faced with brick to match the rest of the courtyard – (and enhance its investment value?).

In 1842, available 'club' accommodation was reduced when, with an £8,000 mortgage, the Society agreed to rebuild Nos. 11 and 12 on the south side of the garden for renting to the Taxing Masters in Chancery. These fine new buildings were completed in 1843 in 'the purest style of James I'.

New trustees were recruited in 1851 (the first for forty years, and just as well as only one of the 1811 trustees was still living) and again in 1875 and April 1884.

*View of the Taxing Master's Office, Staple Inn.*
Lithograph by L. J. Wood, circa 1840
(© Institute of Actuaries)

## CHAPTER SEVEN

Each time they declared that the House of Chancery commonly called Staple Inn was to be conveyed 'to the use of us and our heirs and assigns for ever'[58].

In 1854–1855 a Royal Commission investigated the Inns of Court and Chancery. In its evidence the Society of Staple Inn disclaimed any involvement with the legal profession. Some insight into the gulf which had arisen between Gray's Inn and its 'daughter' Inns is given by the evidence from the Barnard's Inn Treasurer that about 200 years earlier a Reader had come occasionally from Gray's Inn to Barnard's Inn, but 'of what he read about, or who paid him, there is no evidence whatever'[58]. No Reader had been appointed for Staple Inn since 1675. The Commission concluded that the Inns of Chancery were no longer able to make an effective contribution to legal education. The Ancients of Staple Inn were delighted.

The 'club' and 'office' benefits of owning Staple Inn were also becoming less significant. The Roll of Admissions shows 494 new members between 1716 and 1799 (5.9 per annum), but only 87 between 1800 and 1881 (0.9 per annum). The Principal reported to the Royal Commission in 1854 that there were 28 dinners each year, but he almost certainly inflated that figure to satisfy the Commissioners that the members were busy with their own activities and had nothing to do with legal training. In 1855 the Society's membership was the Principal, eight Ancients and twelve juniors. A report in *The Times* states that the number of dinners had fallen to seven or eight a year by the early 1880s, with perhaps up to 40 people present[49].

A picture of Staple Inn in 1882 as a quaint, grey, creaking, old-fashioned place is drawn in two novels written in 1908 and 1989[19,20]. In each a solicitor is involved in a tale of murder and mystery. By then the attractions of Staple Inn as somewhere to live were, for many professional people, severely compromised by the worsening slums, industrialisation, and polluted air around them, and by the prospect of escape to more distant suburbs on improving public transport. The middle classes were turning away from living in the less attractive parts of inner London, of which to many eyes Holborn was one. The clientele for renting residential chambers and joining the dining club was reducing – and London had many dining clubs within easy reach in more prosperous areas.

The one remaining item of value to the members of the Society was their financial investment. After the abolition of the rank of Serjeant-at-Law in 1873, Serjeant's Inn was sold profitably by its owners in 1877. The Principal and Ancients at Staple Inn took their cue from this. As an unincorporated body they had the power to end their existence and retain the proceeds from the sale of the assets. In January 1884 they saw the members of Clement's Inn sell out to one of their number for £65,000.

An economic crisis was developing, business confidence was low, there was considerable social unrest and violence, and the unemployed were protesting in the streets.

Was this the time for them to sell?

CHAPTER EIGHT

# *Under New Management into the Twentieth Century*

### § 8.1 SALE OF STAPLE INN AND THE END OF THE SOCIETY OF STAPLE INN, 1884

On 25 September 1884 the outstanding mortgage on the newly built houses at Nos. 11 and 12 was paid off. On 29 September Staple Inn was sold by the Principal and nine Ancients to G. Trollope and Sons, a firm of builders, for £80,000. The Society of Staple Inn was wound up.

Each Ancient received £8,000, plus money obtained from the sale of fitments, plate and ornaments. The 1882 paintings of the Hall by J. Crowther show at least twelve paintings on the walls, and busts of the twelve Caesars on display. These were sold or taken away by the Ancients, along with tableware and silver.

Tenants of the Inn were able to stay if they wished, and they did so. In 1885 there were solicitors in eight of the ten houses. Other occupants included the Land Registry Office, two architects, a surveyor, a law stationer, a patent officer, an accountant – and Mr Festing. (See section 8.4.)

In 1888 the population was broadly the same, but with four architects and two stationers. Businesses on the road front included a tobacconist in No. 337 High Holborn and possibly a William Stanley shop still in No. 3 Holborn, (photographed there in 1858). Stanley was a prolific inventor, manufacturer and philanthropist, producing mathematical and surveying instruments, and a range of more individual products such as a self-holding double eyeglass. (The ground-floor shops now mark a postal boundary – Nos. 337–338 High Holborn under the two west gables and Nos. 1–4 Holborn under the five gables to the east.)

The occupants of buildings nearby may have had mixed feelings about the prospect of demolition and rebuilding. They included tea merchants, a tailor, artist, boot and shoemaker, ladies' outfitter, milliner, hatter, and writing engraver. In Southampton Row were a linen draper, tailor, tourist's agent, bookseller, jewellers and watchmaker.

*View looking towards east elevation of Staple Inn Hall before its sale in 1884.*
Watercolour by John Crowther, 1882.   (© Guildhall Library, Corporation of London)

## § 8.2 PUBLIC OPINION BEFORE THE AUCTION OF STAPLE INN, 1886

Whether G. Trollope and Sons initially intended to develop the site themselves or to sell it on is unclear. Twenty months passed without much public comment or action, although *The Builder* magazine reported on 29 November 1884 that Staple Inn was said to have been sold to Pickford and Co for conversion to a depot for their removals business. Fortunately this rumour proved untrue.

On 24 June 1886 G. Trollope and Sons sold Nos. 11 and 12 to the south of the garden for £32,000 to the Commissioners of Works and Buildings (who had taken over the lease from the Taxing Masters in Chancery in 1883). The ambience of the south garden was thus put at risk through the split ownership of the buildings around it.

In August 1886 G. Trollope and Sons announced a public auction for the rest of Staple Inn. This provoked expressions of public concern, including a powerful 3,500 word article in *The Times* on 3 November 1886. The article gave a sympathetic account of the Inn's history. It deplored the plan for it to be sold by auction for demolition and rebuilding 'as stacks of modern shops and offices'[49]. It argued passionately (in the language of the day) for it to be preserved, if necessary by the State taking it over.

The article was unsure whether to aim its fire at G. Trollope and Sons or at the former Principal and Ancients (in case they were using Trollope to test the public pulse).

> It is absurd that the beneficiaries of one particular time and generation should take upon themselves to appropriate the body of the trust, to put an end to the institution of which they are the temporary guardians, and to enlarge their private means with the proceeds of its lands and goods … There is a strong case for stopping this trafficking in quasi-public property… No time should be lost in extending the protecting hand of the State to property which the natural guardians are deserting'[49].

That rebuilding was in G. Trollope and Sons' mind is evidenced by advertisements for the auction. One refers to the 'important freehold building site, comprising Staple Inn…', another to the 'valuable freehold building site…'[48].

*The Times* article had some impact. On 19 November there was a meeting at the Guildhall of the Court of Common Council, led by the Mayor, which received a deputation from the Commons Preservation Society and the Society for the Protection of Ancient Buildings. They urged the Corporation to purchase Staple Inn, partly as an investment (able to earn '3% p.a.') and partly as an act of public spirit. They suggested a purchase price of £53–£55,000 to enable G. Trollope and Sons to recoup the £48,000 balance of their £80,000 outlay and to make a profit.

The debate was lively, with strong views for and against:

> While men are starving in London the Corporation can better employ its money than in buying Staple Inn[50].

The vote showed a large majority in favour of referring the proposal to the Coal, Corn and Finance Committee for follow up. (It is unclear to what extent the Committee was moved by a suggestion that to reject it would be a poor compliment to the previous Mayor, Alderman Sir John Staples.)

Meanwhile the Prudential Assurance Company, which was becoming massively involved with the British public through its insurance business, was also considering making a bid. Founded in 1848, with the image of Prudence for the company seal, the Prudential pioneered a new form of life insurance in 1854, selling penny policies to individuals so successfully that by 1905 they insured one third of the UK population. Their reasons for considering a bid for Staple Inn were various – for commercial investment; to protect the side of the road opposite their new headquarters from undesirable development; to support the public interest and promote their name by preserving these historic buildings; and perhaps also conscious that they hoped to demolish nearby Furnival's Inn later to make way for new buildings. The 'social responsibility' reason was clearly present in their Board Minutes at the time[38], and in a letter to *The Times* in late August 1905[39].

The Prudential Board authorised a bid of up to £80,000.

## § 8.3 AUCTION OF STAPLE INN, NOVEMBER 1886

On 26 November 1886 the auction took place in a large crowded room at the Mart, Tokenhouse Yard, north of Bank. The description of the property referred to the current rental income providing a return for the investor 'pending the maturing of a building scheme'[51]. Various standard conditions were laid down plus the requirement to maintain a minimum 8 feet wide passage somewhere between the Holborn road and the southern exit from the property. Reference was made to Staple Inn being extra-parochial, and the tenants paying 'Inn dues' for the rates.

The auctioneer tried to establish the special status of the Inn and talk up its value, commenting on the high level of public interest in it. He suggested it might be suitable as a Church House, a law school, a museum, or even a central depot for the Midland or Great Northern Railways. There is 'no end to the valuable purposes to which the site might be put'. He argued that it would fetch £112,000 if the same price per square foot was applied as in the Serjeant's Inn sale nine years earlier, and that it was worth more.

Someone asked if the City Corporation was negotiating its purchase. A reply from the floor said that 'they cannot get the Coal and Wine duties'. The auctioneer said that should not stop them raising the money to make a bid. A solicitor protested that the sale was neither legal nor moral, and that it should be referred to Parliament and perhaps the Court of Chancery.

Undeterred the auctioneer sought to start the bidding at £112,000. There was a deafening silence. Requests for bids of £100,000, £90,000, £85,000 and £80,000 were similarly ignored. Someone then offered £50,000. With suitable hesitations ten further bids each £1,000 higher raised the offer to £60,000. At this point the auctioneer made an impassioned call for sensible bids from the Corporation, the Government, the 'aesthetics', or 'Gog and Magog'. Thus inspired, further £1,000 bids took the price to £67,000, followed by four £250 increases.

Reluctantly, the auctioneer's hammer fell on the twenty-second bid, at £68,000. A firm of solicitors had made the successful bid on behalf of the Prudential. They were still well within the Board's approved ceiling. G. Trollope and Sons made a profit of £20,000 less expenses on their original £80,000 outlay.

The reluctance of companies to make full commercial development bids in the face of public concerns about the sale may be seen as a turning point in England in the views and influence of the public on the fate of old buildings.

## § 8.4 THE INSTITUTE OF ACTUARIES RENTS STAPLE INN HALL, 1887

Six days after the auction, on 2 December 1886, the Prudential requested the architect Alfred Waterhouse to survey Staple Inn and advise on the best method of putting the property in a desirable state of repair without interfering with its characteristic features. Waterhouse was responsible for the design of many of the Prudential's buildings, including their headquarters on the other side of Holborn road.

By 9 December 1886 the Prudential and the Institute of Actuaries had agreed terms for a yearly tenancy of the Hall and the two adjoining rooms, for an inclusive rent of £250 p.a. The Prudential reserved the right to use the Hall four times each year (later revised to ten evenings each year).

Such speed of decision-making was admirable! It seems likely that the Institute, which had been looking for new accommodation since October, was part of discussions leading up to the Prudential's bid. A letter from the Prudential to the Institute dated 9 December shows that their Board had already agreed the details of the tenancy by that date[44]. A paper prepared by the Institute General Purposes Committee which was discussed by the Institute Council on 9 December (and probably sent out before the meeting?) also shows evidence of study of the Staple Inn accommodation and of discussions with the Prudential about the terms of a lease[44].

The formal transfer to the Institute was sealed in May 1887. At the Institute's Annual General Meeting in the Hall on 4 June 1887 the Prudential were commended warmly for the liberal spirit in which they had agreed the terms. The Institute spent £208 making 'the requisite House arrangements', and a celebratory dinner took place in the Hall. Its membership was then 484, just 5% of

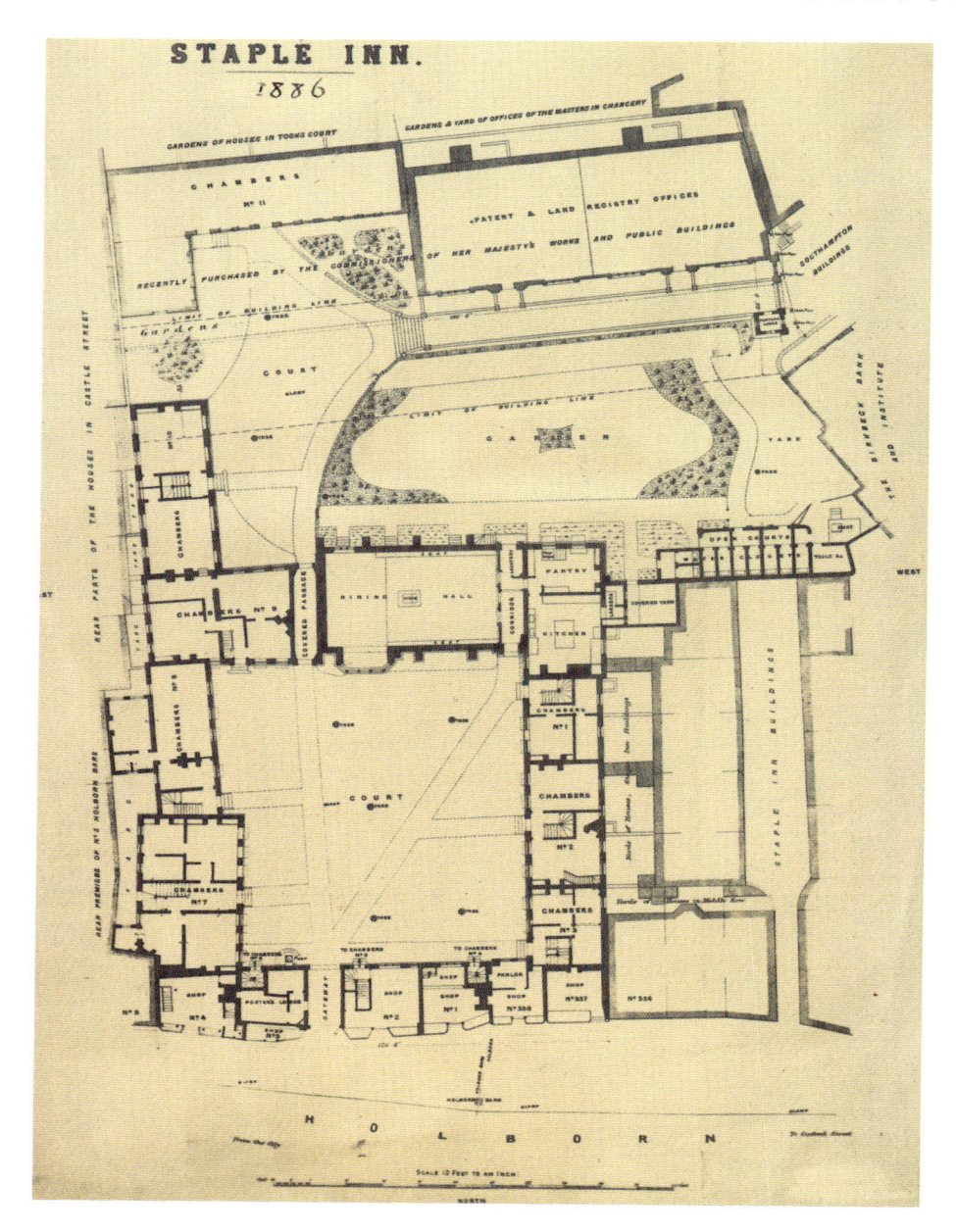

*Plan of Staple Inn in 1886.* (© Archives of Prudential plc)

the membership a hundred years later, and its annual subscription income was £969.

So ended a 35-year period in which the Institute shared accommodation with the Statistical Society, from 1852 at 12 St James's Square, from 1874 at King's College, and from 1884 at 9 Adelphi Terrace. For its first 4 years from 1848 the Institute was housed at 12 Chatham Place, Blackfriars, with the Family Endowment Society.

### § 8.5 1887 RESTORATION WORK

The restoration work in 1887 led by Alfred Waterhouse was notable for removing the plaster that had hidden the timbers of the Holborn front since the Great Fire of 1666, and for reinstating the Tudor bow windows which had miraculously been stored unharmed in the cellars for the same period. The Prudential decided to press ahead with the restoration despite objections to the removal of the plaster façade from the Society for the Protection of Ancient Buildings. Perhaps the Society was flexing its muscles after its formation in 1877 – one of its formal concerns was that medieval walls should not be scraped down to their original state[54].

Improvements to the rest of the site were relatively modest. The Hall was disturbed as little as Waterhouse judged prudent, the only important alteration being the insertion of tie-rods to each of the five principal beams in the roof. Paint was removed from the oak panelling in the Hall.

There were plane trees in the courtyard and a tobacco business in the west ground-floor shop[49], which has continued, through various owners including John Brumfit, to today's *Ye Olde Tobacco Shoppe* at 337–338 High Holborn.

The Prudential also bought the site next to Staple Inn, commissioning Waterhouse to design and construct Staple Inn Buildings. This 1901 combination of terracotta and Gothic-inspired decorations is on a site made more attractive by the demolition of Middle Row 34 years earlier. Waterhouse wanted buff terracotta, but the Prudential insisted on red to match their headquarters, to preserve their corporate image.

# CHAPTER NINE
## *Twentieth-century Triumphs over Adversity, and Rejuvenation*

### § 9.1 THE ACTUARIES AND EARLY IMPROVEMENTS TO THE BUILDINGS

The 1887 restoration left Staple Inn in its traditional, relatively spartan style of comfort. The Hall was lit by gas from side brackets and two hanging chandeliers lit by a taper on a long pole. Heating came from a stove on a stone slab in the middle of the Hall (previously an open fire). All seats were in hard wood. Water came from the courtyard pump.

New facilities were introduced, gradually, as tenants sought them. After a plaintive call from the Institute of Actuaries about the damp 'injuring the books in the Library', the Prudential agreed 'to install an apparatus with the necessary furnace, etc, for heating the Hall by means of hot pipes'[44]. The new central heating was installed in 1890.

The first electric lights in the Hall appeared in 1896, replacing the gaslights. (Edison built the world's first power station at 57 Holborn Viaduct in 1883, demonstrating the benefits of electric lighting at the Old Bailey and the General Post Office nearby. It closed in 1886, but many small stations were built within a few years.)

The new century was anticipated with the arrival of the first typewriter in 1899. A domestic telephone was installed in 1900, followed after a four-year struggle by the first public telephone in 1902 – some splendidly tidy actuarial minds had objected to the sight of messy wires. (The first telephone exchange in London had opened in Lombard Street in 1879.) In 1911 superior metal filament lamps were introduced[44].

Seating in the Hall was on chairs along the side walls, in parliamentary style, in two rows when attendance was high, with bookcases behind. As attendance at

*Earliest surviving photograph of Staple Inn Hall in the 1890s.*

(© Institute of Actuaries)

meetings increased the seats were turned to face the dais. At other times the Hall was laid out for student classes, or with tables for examinations. The Institute of Actuaries' Students Society was formed in 1910 to help students prepare for examinations, to increase their professional knowledge, and to give them practice and confidence in public speaking. Never had the legal students of the distant past faced such intense examination scrutiny.

In 1903 the Institute offices expanded into the new Staple Inn Buildings through a connecting corridor, and to the 'New Hall' there. With the extra 'Secretaries' Room, Cloakroom and Actuaries' Examination Hall (about 38 by 32 feet) a new 21-year lease was signed at an annual rent of £600. There was early flirtation with renting the Hall or rooms to outside bodies. In 1909 the policy was established that this should only be allowed in a few special cases, but in the war conditions from 1915 more external lettings were agreed. In 1919 a man was killed cleaning the New Hall windows, a compensation claim being settled in Court.

Other tenants elsewhere round the courtyard also adapted their rooms to new needs.

The overall impact of Staple Inn on many was still that of an Oxbridge College, with staircases leading to offices and residential accommodation. It retained in tangible form the 'university' image first expressed five hundred years earlier.

## § 9.2 1914-1936

There is no record of damage at Staple Inn in the First World War, although Lincoln's Inn Chapel nearby was damaged by a bomb dropped from a German Zeppelin in 1915. In the same year the City of London Volunteer Corps made their headquarters in Staple Inn. In 1916 some bookcases were moved from the main Hall to the Examination Hall, and in 1919 the rest were stored in the Cloakroom. Later a Library was formed near the Hall. The Institute's lease was renewed on similar terms in 1924.

People still lived in Staple Inn. Under the heading 'Discovery in Holborn', an article in *The Morning Post* on 18 February 1930 claimed a great find in the south garden pond, where 'in lordly and solitary splendour swims London's last carp, a living link with gracious Tudor days'. A letter to the Editor three days later regretfully denied the 'living link' with Tudor days. It explained that the writer and his brother, as young children living in No. 6 Staple Inn, had been persuaded by their governess to move their numerous fish from the glass tank in the house to the pond in the 'Sun Gardens' for the summer. When the family moved away they left the carp behind, and the severe frosts of 1916 killed all but two of them. One later committed suicide by leaping out of the pond, leaving the one survivor. He, however, was 'a maximum of 18 years of age'.

In 1919 the Institute of Actuaries admitted women for the first time as members, although numbers in the early years were small. Dorothy Spiers, the first woman to qualify as a Fellow in 1923, was the first woman to open an Institute Sessional Meeting in the Hall in 1926.

A Latin inscription on a stone in the courtyard paving, '*Puteus oppletus*', states that a well was filled there in 1922. A few yards away there is a circular seat with nothing inside it. A photograph in T.C. Worsfold's book shows a tree in that place with a similar circular seat round it[58]. It seems one day the tree started to sink into the well, necessitating its removal and the well's closure. Another perhaps complementary story is that a child fell into the well, leading to its closure.

Also in 1922 the failure of a lintel over a window revealed that the Hall oak roof was severely damaged by death watch beetle. The timbers were treated, some were replaced, and a steel frame was fitted between the ceiling and the roof slates. The Institute President, knowing the roof to be eighteen inches higher than before, explained that:

> a great deal of concealed woodwork had been replaced by steel girders, which were continued upwards between the ceiling and roof… The beams that were visible were now bolted to the steel girders. The result was that the roof was now supporting these venerable beams which for nearly 400 years had supported the roof[44].

*Staple Inn courtyard showing tree covering well.*
Photograph for T. Cato Worsfold, 1903.
(© Henry Bumpus, publisher)

Car parking was allowed in the courtyard during the 1926 General Strike. However the notice in the inner archway of the Holborn street entrance has no doubt been obeyed meticulously over the centuries:

> The PORTER Has Orders To
> Prevent Old Clothes Men & Others
> From Calling Articles For Sale. Also
> Rude Children Playing &c.
> No Horses Allowed Within This Inn.

There was a Staple Inn Publishing Company in 1927. In 1929 the actuaries leased extra rooms for Committee Meetings and for the Assistant Secretary. In 1932 former Institute President W.P. Phelps donated a new seventeen feet long refectory Council table and chairs. The table was based on an Elizabethan example, probably from Moreton Hall in Cheshire, its top made from Windsor Forest oak, two of its six legs nearly 400 years old from another Inn's beam. The frieze under the edge of the table was copied from the carving under the Hall gallery. At the same time the Hall lighting was improved with cornice lamps.

In 1936 the post-prandial nap of the Institute of Actuaries' Secretary (I jest of course) was rudely disturbed one day when the wire cable supporting the huge weights which drove the clocks broke. The weights were at the top of their run and descended from their full height through the cellar to a depth of three feet in the earth. The Secretary reported an explosion, but was unable to identify what or where it had been[8].

§ 9.3 REBUILDING THE TUDOR FRONTAGE, 1936–1939
Perhaps inspired by the clock incident, the Prudential surveyed the buildings for possible repair in November 1936. High drama followed. Almost every timber along the Holborn front was found to be fractured, rotten or consumed by beetles. The remaining wood was 'as brittle as a lump of coal', said Mr Coombe, the surveyor. Some chimney-stacks were nearly two feet out of plumb[8].

*Staple Inn looking deceptively secure in 1930. Restoration to prevent its near-collapse from beetle infestation would become an emergency in 1936.*
Prudential Assurance Company Calendar of 1930.  (© Archives of Prudential plc)

The Georgian back wall facing the courtyard proved to be no better than the Tudor front. It was revealed to be only 9 inches thick, with its two 4.5 inch skins largely unbonded. In that fragile state they had stood to a height of over 35 feet, 80 feet long, with no buttress or support, for at least 110 years. The wall had been built in 1826, or earlier, to match the design of the other courtyard developments and hide the 1586 rear elevation. 'How it stood so long, I don't know', said Mr Coombe[8]. Clearly the occupants had for long learnt to move about their work with stealthy tread.

Equally remarkable was the architects' discovery by the architects and builders, E.W. Spiller that:

we have not found any trace of comprehensive works of restoration, although here and there individual timbers have been repaired from time to time[8].

The 1586–1589 structure had stood proud for 350 years.

The restoration required enormous care and skill. It needed delicate shoring, daily inspection of vital wedges, inserting a new steel frame inside the old shell with all its peculiar shapes, replacing the timbers, and providing a more modern interior layout for the offices and shops, including the installation of a water supply and lavatories. The pump in the courtyard was no longer the only source of water.

For three years the public picked their way carefully through props and hoardings along the pavement. Approval was given by the Society for the Preservation of Ancient Buildings and the Royal Fine Arts Committee.

In their continuing public-spirited way the Prudential paid the £48,500 restoration cost. This stimulated a letter to the Company from the London Society expressing their very great appreciation:

It is not every owner who would act in so enlightened a manner and all who are interested in the preservation of the little that remains of London before the Fire must feel a debt of gratitude to the Prudential[38].

*Eighteenth-century lady's shoe patten discovered in 1938 – once protecting finer footwear from the filth of Holborn Street or warding off evil spirits in the building?*
(© Archives of Prudential plc)

Happily virtue had some reward since the shops and offices proved attractive, and increased rentals secured a reasonable return of 5.1% p.a. on the overall investment in the front buildings. The long-established Clarkson (scientific instruments) and Brumfit (tobacco) businesses were in the two west shops. The upper eastern part of the Holborn frontage was leased by the Institute of Actuaries in 1937 for the Actuarial Tuition Service, a Students' Room, and space for further expansion.

No. 10 needed a new end wall, roof and buttresses. Repairs to the other houses were less dramatic. Outside in the street some of the eyesore trolley-bus poles were removed in 1937.

The rebuilding brought to light several parchments, a seventeenth-century candle-snuffer, a shilling coin with the mint mark of a Crescent dated 1587–1589[41], and a hidden shoe patten*.

One parchment, dated 1633, records payments to be made in a lawsuit. Another, dated 5 May 1638, seems to refer to the same lawsuit. William Phylpe complains that following arrest two years before at the suit of Joanne Gable he paid to her attorney all sums due. Later the attorney had him arrested again after he refused to pay more money, and obtained a judgement for the sale of his goods to the value of £7. This was sworn before Fr. Crawley, presumably Sir Francis of doubtful reputation as a Judge in the Court of Common Pleas. (See section 5.5.) Another parchment was the four-page treatise in the Presbyterian interest in favour of religious toleration, probably dated 1650s. (See section 5.8.)

### § 9.4 THE SECOND WORLD WAR, AND DISASTER IN 1944

At the start of the 1939 war the stained glass in the Hall was removed to the cellars and the more valuable books in the Institute's Library were taken elsewhere for safekeeping. The Institute's minute books from 1848 were stored safely with their bankers, and also microfilmed. Copies of publications were held in at least two different buildings. Because the Hall was not blacked out meetings could only take place in daylight hours. Institute staff moved to offices provided by the Prudential, and the 1941 examinations were held in an air-raid shelter there.

---

*A shoe patten was an overshoe on a high metal ring. Advice from the Victoria and Albert Museum and from the Northampton Central Museum (home of the largest collection of boots and shoes in Britain) dates this to the early years of the eighteenth century. 'Its decorative stitching on the band to tie over the foot appears typical of that used to decorate the clog overshoes made to match shoes.' More pointed toes were introduced from 1730. It is a rare survival, and was 'definitely worn by a woman from the middle classes', possibly for country wear as much as town. Its purpose was to lift the shoe above the filth and mire of the street.

The used shoe patten was possibly concealed deliberately as were many others over several centuries, for superstitious reasons. 'The builders' sacrifice' left in prominent buildings graduated through time from human sacrifice to animals and to objects, and especially shoes. It may have been intended to protect the building and people against evil forces, to attract good forces, to promote fertility, to protect the spirits of the dead, or more sinisterly to gain control over a person by sealing up their shoes which were sometimes slashed. Only well worn shoes were concealed. This may just have been sensible economy, since shoes were expensive, or may reflect the wish to preserve the spirit of the wearer, since the shoe is the only item of clothing which retains something of the shape of the wearer's body.

CHAPTER NINE

*Bomb damage of 1944 – yet the roof structure lies largely intact.*
(© Institute of Actuaries)

*Bomb damage of 1944 – looking across the garden to No. 1, the Hall and No. 10.*
Published in *Journal of the Institute of Actuaries (1946)* **72**. (© Institute of Actuaries)

Fire-watching rotas were arranged at the Inn. In April 1941 incendiary bombs hit the courtyard and some buildings, but the fire was put out quickly. Weeks later incendiary and high explosive bombs damaged the dome of the bell tower. St Andrew's Church down the road was badly damaged, as were the Middle and Inner Temples. Early, distant flying bombs broke some plain glass in the Hall.

Staple Inn's occupants took shelter during air raids in the Hall basement. The deep shelter at Chancery Lane underground station, opened in 1943, was used as a rest place for off-duty servicemen. Several hundred were provided with bed and breakfast every night, staffed from 8.00 a.m. to 8.00 p.m. by six women from a pool of 54 Prudential volunteers. The advent of V1 flying bombs added to the sense of hazard, shattering hundreds of windows in buildings near the Inn.

At about 7.30 p.m. on Thursday 24 August 1944 a flying bomb exploded in the garden by the goldfish pool.

The Hall, Nos. 1 and 10 and parts of the Patent Office buildings to the south of the garden were demolished. Other buildings were considerably damaged, including some in the courtyard and Southampton Buildings. In Staple Inn Nos.

7–9 were least affected. The roof of the Hall fell to rest on the floor, with the basement below intact. The steel frame that had been fitted in 1923 between the ceiling and the roof caused the roof to fall to the ground largely in one piece.

The 1937–1939 steel frame of the Holborn front enabled those buildings to escape relatively unscathed, as they had 277 years earlier in the Great Fire. If the frame had not been fitted so carefully six years earlier, the buildings would almost certainly have collapsed beyond repair. There is an account of a huge blast of air rushing through the windows from the courtyard to the street beyond[57].

A lady who had worked in the Inn for 40 years was killed on her way to the basement shelter. She had commented a few weeks earlier that she expected to end her days in the Inn's service. The Inn Porter and Night Porter heard the flying bomb's engine stop and just made it to the safety of the Lodge. The Porter's wife and little son were in the basement shelter and reported the explosion as 'terrific'. Some American soldiers helped them out, unhurt. The Porter said that 'the locks on all the doors in the building were wrenched off and some party walls in Nos. 8 and 5 had collapsed'[27].

Frank Guaschi, actuary, was kicking a football as a young boy just behind the Prudential buildings across the road from Staple Inn when:

> I looked up to see the 'doodlebug' coming from the general direction of Clerkenwell… All at once the engine stopped and we threw ourselves to the ground. There was an enormous explosion…We leapt up and ran down Gray's Inn Road to see a cloud of dust arising from behind the old Tudor buildings in front of Staple Inn. I must have been one of the first on the scene, and beheld a huge pile of rubble, with the roof barely recognisable sitting on top of it. Staple Inn was no more[22].

Residents who had remained in the Inn until then had to move elsewhere, and office work was seriously disrupted. Institute of Actuaries General and Council Meetings took place at the Chartered Insurance Institute offices in Aldermanbury after early help from the Prudential and the Law Society.

The Institute celebrated its centenary at the CII offices in 1948, with the promise of return to Staple Inn still over the horizon.

§ 9.5 REBUILDING AND RETURN, 1954–1955

Plans for rebuilding were prepared soon after the war ended, but did not top the priority list until March 1954. Then Staple Inn Hall and Nos. 1, 2, 3, 9 and 10 were completely rebuilt, and No. 8 partly rebuilt by Sir Edward Maufe and Sir Robert McAlpine and Sons for the long-suffering Prudential. Much of the cost was met by the War Damage Commission. Maufe had also restored the Middle Temple and Gray's Inn, and was made an Honorary Master of the Bench of Gray's Inn in 1951.

The buildings were reconstructed largely as they had been before, although the internal framework of the Hall was now of reinforced concrete, and the post-war shortage of materials caused various short cuts in the fine detail. The hammer beam trusses were still splendidly and mysteriously ornamental. New oak panelling was designed from a panelled room (of circa 1603) exhibited at the Victoria and Albert Museum. Special 2.4-inch bricks of the size used in the old Hall were obtained for the exterior, and Westmoreland roof slates of varying size matched the originals. Extensive grouting was needed on some house walls since hollows had formed between many bricks.

There is a generally held view that the Hall's roof trusses were made largely with new wood, with only one rescued piece reused over the gallery with the original carved pendants. There is, however, an authoritative article in *English Historic Carpentry* by C.A. Hewitt in 1980 arguing that probably most of the moulded components of the roof were reassembled from the original roof, and that if not 'it represents an unrivalled antique faking'[25]. The roof had, after all, fallen more or less in one piece to the floor. I like to go with Hewitt's opinion.

The carving on the old oak screen was reproduced on the wall panelling under the gallery. On the dais the splendid Lidstone Council table replaced that presented by Phelps, which had been destroyed by the bomb.

The Library and office adjacent to the Hall, where the kitchen used to be,

## CHAPTER NINE

*The Council Chamber created in 1955 next to Staple Inn Hall.*
(© Institute of Actuaries)

*The head of the mace acquired in 1816 for Hutton Wood, Principal 1814–1817, bears the date '1553' when the Society of Staple Inn adopted the woolsack as its symbol.*
(© Institute of Actuaries)

were replaced by a single Council Chamber, with access to the Hall through three carved double doors. This Chamber includes an original Elizabethan stone carving on the right of the fireplace, previously buried as infill rubble in a courtyard wall. The bronze war memorial listing the Institute's 88 members who lost their lives in the First World War was retrieved largely undamaged, and is displayed today in the Council Chamber alongside a similar memorial for the 42 members who died in the Second World War. Also displayed are a carved representation of the Institute's Coat of Arms over the fireplace, oak panels with the names of the Institute's Presidents, and a selection of gifts, prizes and medals.

All three clock dials were restored, with the original movement intact. The bell in the cupola was replaced. A replica of the fountain was placed in the original position in the garden. The silver head of the mace was retrieved from the ruins and attached to a new silver-mounted staff, a gift from the Students' Society. This mace had belonged to the Ancients of Staple Inn since 1816, and was presented to the Institute of Actuaries by the Prudential in 1923. An inscription on it refers to the 'Ancient Society of Staple Inn, 1553', which is probably when the woolsack symbol, also inscribed on the original mace, was first formally adopted. (See section 4.10.)

Other survivors of the bomb were busts of distinguished actuaries John Finlaison, Sir George Francis Hardy and Thomas Bond Sprague. A statue of John Napier was presented by the Faculty of Actuaries to replace one that was destroyed.

Also rebuilt in 1954–1955 were the offices of the Patent Office on the south side of the garden. Most regrettably no attempt was made to recreate the former architecture and ambience 'in the purest style of James I'. With a crude parapet in place of the shaped gables, 'a ruthlessly utilitarian section in nasty cheap cream brick', according to Bradley and Pevsner[5], replaced the bombed wing, dominating the garden in which the children used to play.

In May 1955 there was a formal reopening ceremony for Staple Inn, televised by the BBC. The Prudential's Chairman, Sir Frank Morgan, said that it was open

*Stained glass donated by John Spencer in 1958 bearing the Institute crest granted by the Privy Council in 1956.*

(© Institute of Actuaries)

to debate whether this could be regarded as a suitable investment for a life insurance company, but that it was a nice contrast to most of the company's investments:

> The fact that we have bought it, restored it, preserved it and now have re-created it may be set off against the fact that another famous Inn was entirely demolished in order to build the best part of our head office[32].

He referred to Furnival's Inn across the road, demolished in 1897.

In 1958 actuary John Spencer donated a stained glass panel depicting the Institute's Coat of Arms, granted in 1956, to mark the 1955 rebuilding. This is the central upper panel in the third south window. It displays the Institute's motto 'Certum ex incertis'.

Many former tenants returned to their offices. The Institute of Actuaries reoccupied the Hall and neighbouring offices, with its own reopening ceremony on 22 September 1955. On the road-front tobacconists were in the two west shops, Nos. 337–338, and jewellers in No. 3, both businesses, with different owners (Sherringtons and Sanford Bros.) still there today. The other ground-floor shops, Nos. 1, 2 and 4, have had shorter tenancies – recently tailors, outfitters, opticians, confectioners, and teas and coffees.

Further down the road, St Andrew's Church was restored in 1961 with pulpit, font and organ from the chapel of Coram's eighteenth-century Foundling Hospital.

### § 9.6 CITY OF LONDON BOUNDARIES INCLUDE STAPLE INN, 1994

On 1 April 1994 as part of the first major changes to its boundaries for more than 700 years, the City of London boundaries were extended to include Staple Inn. This was not a long-delayed triumph of the City over the Queen, following the struggle for control that the City lost in the thirteenth century, but was boundary rationalisation with Camden Borough.

There was a fitting symbolic recognition of the newcomer to the City when the garden to the south of the Hall won the City's 'best-kept small garden' award in 1995.

By then, in 1991, barristers had returned to Staple Inn, as 'Staple Inn Chambers', the first for over a hundred years.

### § 9.7 REFURBISHMENT INCLUDING STAPLE INN HALL, 1993–1998

After 1955 improvements continued to be made to the buildings. Special rooms were developed in Nos. 1 and 3 for use by the Institute President and in honour of distinguished actuaries Elderton, Lidstone, Phelps and Redington. The Institute celebrated its 125th anniversary in 1973 with 244 members present and 60 overseas guests. Closed-circuit television was fitted in the Council Chamber and Redington Room in 1980 for overflow from the Hall as larger numbers attended meetings.

In 1985, to mark its 75th Anniversary, the Institute of Actuaries Students' Society presented the two stained glass panels in the lower central panels of the north window near the entrance from the courtyard. Made by Goddard & Gibbs, one formally records the Institute's 1884 Royal Charter and the Students'

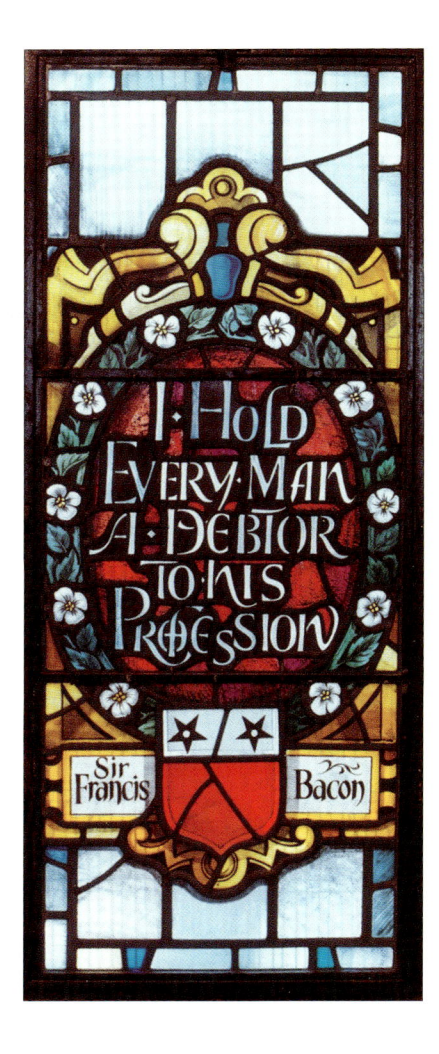

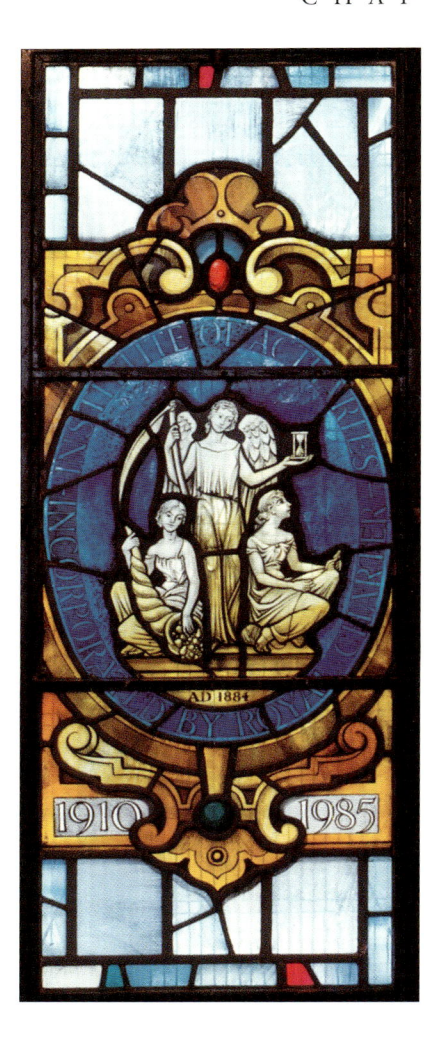

# CHAPTER NINE

Society's life from 1910 to 1985. The other quotes the first nine words from a statement by Sir Francis Bacon of Gray's Inn in *The Elements of the Common Law* (1596) from which actuaries find inspiration in sustaining their enormous voluntary effort to maintain and develop their profession:

> I hold every man a debtor to his profession, from the which as men of course do seek to receive countenance and profit, so ought they of duty to endeavour themselves by way of amends to be a help and ornament thereunto.

Major changes came with complete modernisation of the offices in Nos. 1 and 3 from 1993–1996, and refurbishment of the Hall, Council Chamber and related basement in 1996–1997. This both restored the ambience of the Hall more closely to its original Elizabethan style and modernised the facilities.

The texture of the oak panelling was enhanced, the oak floor boards, with sound-deadening fixings, were sanded to achieve the original lighter colour, and dais panels and neo-classical pediment provided visual focus at the higher end of the Hall. Period lighting sconces and chandeliers were part of a sophisticated lighting scheme. The roof trusses were polished to highlight the remarkable arch-braced hammer-beams and baroque carved detail. The stained glass windows and stone dressings were cleaned and restored.

The building services were significantly upgraded to provide flexible environmental and audio-visual facilities. Improved lighting and a new heating system were installed. For the first time access throughout the neighbouring office building was enabled for those with impaired mobility in wheelchairs.

The refurbishment was carried out at the expense of the Institute of Actuaries, firmly established as long-term tenants, under Martin Ashley Architects in close co-operation with the Corporation of London, English Heritage, The Museum of London and the Prudential. The Hall was reopened by the Lord Mayor in February 1997.

The quality of Staple Inn's buildings is recognised in their official listing. The Holborn road front buildings are listed Grade I, including Nos. 4, 5 and 6 and

*Windows designed by John Lawson and presented by the Institute of Actuaries Students' Society on its 75th anniversary in 1985.*
(© Institute of Actuaries)

# TWENTIETH-CENTURY TRIUMPHS OVER ADVERSITY, AND REJUVENATION

*Tapestry by Jennie Moncur, presented to adorn the Hall by actuary Alan Fishman in 1998.*
(© Institute of Actuaries)

the courtyard water pump, dated 1937, attached to No. 6. Listed Grade II are the Hall and attached railings, Nos. 1, 2, 3, 7, 8, 9 and 10, and the nineteenth-century lamppost in the courtyard.

In December 1997 a tapestry measuring 3.2 by 2.5 metres was hung high on the wall at the east end of the Hall. Designed by Jennie Moncur, it includes Tudor roses and the woolsack to reflect the history of the Hall, motifs of the Faculty of Actuaries and Institute of Actuaries, and actuarial symbols to help maintain interest in the unlikely event that a session in the Hall fails to command attention. The tapestry includes a fish to honour its donor, actuary Alan Fishman[28].

Four new stained glass panels were added in 1998, bringing the total in the Hall to 54. These were gifts to mark the Institute's 150th Anniversary from the American Academy of Actuaries, the Society of Actuaries in America, the Canadian Institute of Actuaries, and the Faculty of Actuaries in Scotland.

Also donated in 1998 were two wood coats-of-arms. One was from the Worshipful Company of Actuaries, placed on the north-west elevation beam with the motto '*Experience foretells*'. The Worshipful Company became the 91st Livery Company of the City of London in 1979. The other coat-of-arms was donated by actuary Kenneth Ayers, former Sheriff of the City of London, with the motto '*Honour in sincerity and tolerance*', placed on the south-west elevation beam near the balcony.

The cleaning and restoration of the stained glass windows, and the new gifts, dramatically improve the Hall's impact. It now provides a magical centre for the other fine features of this lovely place, a shining jewel in the heart of London – so different from the grey, old-fashioned perceptions of a hundred years earlier.

CHAPTER NINE

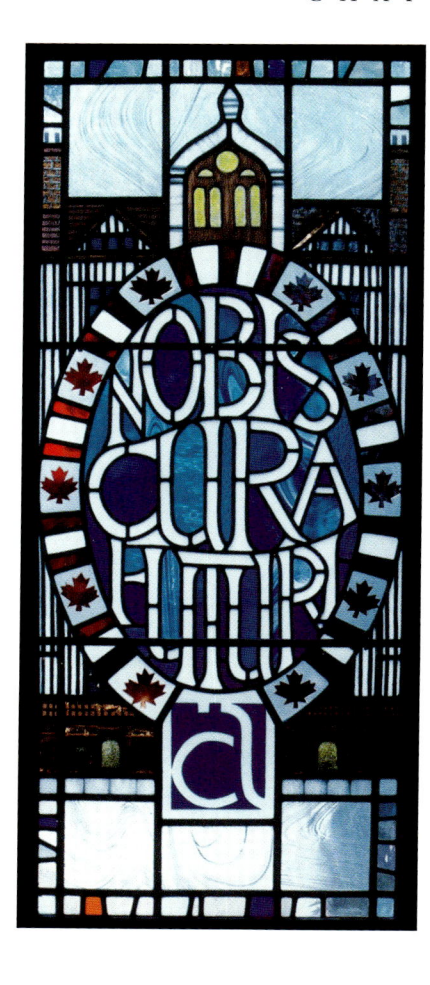

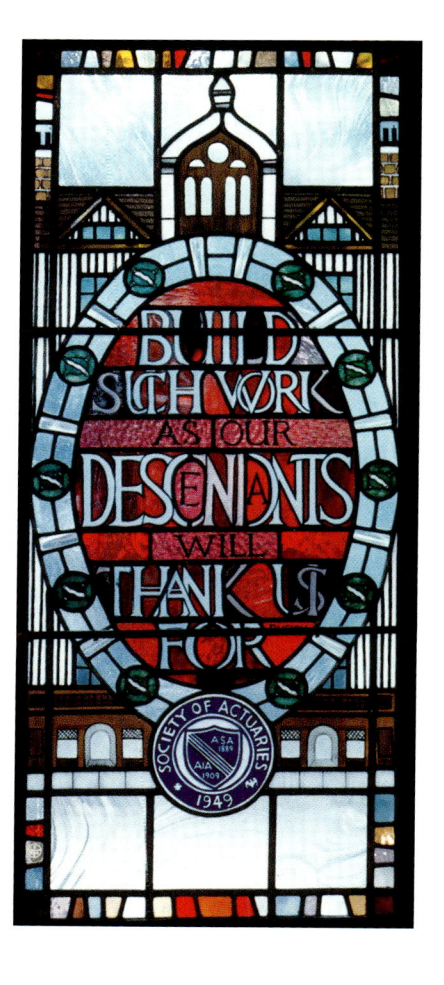

*Window presented by the American Academy of Actuaries on the 150th anniversary of the Actuarial Profession in Britain.*

(© Institute of Actuaries)

*Window presented by the Canadian Institute of Actuaries on the 150th anniversary of the Actuarial Profession in Britain.*

(© Institute of Actuaries)

*Window presented by the Society of Actuaries (of the United States) on the 150th anniversary of the Actuarial Profession in Britain.*

(© Institute of Actuaries)

*The Faculty of Actuaries (est. 1856) with whom the Institute now works jointly also presented its crest on the 150th anniversary.*

(© Institute of Actuaries)

## § 9.8 THE ACTUARIES AND TWENTIETH-CENTURY REJUVENATION OF STAPLE INN

The story of Staple Inn in the last century has been shaped by two significant organisations. Its long-term care has been secure with the Prudential, determined to maintain this historic setting while earning a reasonable return on investment. Its long-term use has been rejuvenated by tenants in the shops and offices, and especially by the Institute of Actuaries.

The Institute's membership has increased from 484 in 1887 to 2,105 (848 Fellows) in 1955 and to 10,756 (5,129 Fellows) in 2000. In partnership with the Faculty of Actuaries in Scotland it plays a key role in the nation's financial affairs, especially regarding pensions, insurance and investment. Apart from the war years there has been steady growth in the profession's activities at Staple Inn, with a gallop in the last ten years. It now occupies, in addition to the Hall, not just two rooms but about half the total office space around the courtyard – all of Nos. 1–3, parts of Nos. 9 and 10, and extensive basement areas. During the 1990s the Institute invested about £2 million improving its facilities at the Inn. About 40 Institute staff work there, and hundreds of volunteer actuaries visit to contribute and to learn.

The Hall is no longer just a 'dining room' (see 1886 plan), but an active business, education, conference and social centre. Actuaries' meetings by day and evening attract up to several hundred participants, some with distinguished outside speakers. Twice a year graduation ceremonies are attended by several dozen new Fellows and twice as many family and friends. Splendid dinners mark key actuarial occasions, both of the Institute and of the Worshipful Company. Past Institute President Stewart Lyon composed a sung Grace for one such evening, and other forms of music are performed from the gallery. External groups hire the Hall and its facilities for Annual General Meetings, product launches, business presentations, conferences, and social gatherings. At weekends the Hall, courtyard and garden provide a high quality venue for wedding receptions and anniversary parties – there is a wedding reception on most Saturdays throughout the year. On recent 'London Open House' weekends, when places of national interest are encouraged to open their doors to the public, more than a thousand people have come to admire the courtyard and the Hall. Staple Inn is on the standard trail for some London walking tours.

If Charles Dickens were writing now he would surely find a more lively symbolism to characterise Staple Inn than 'a little nook' with 'smoky, deluded, crippled sparrows twittering on smoky trees'. The image of 'cotton in his ears, and velvet soles on his boots' might remain, but he would surely reflect, instead of a 'prisonous look', a sense of significant purpose, activity, comradeship and laughter. Birds are still there around the Inn, but so are people, walking, sitting, chatting together, enjoying a sandwich, reading, confiding in their mobile phones.

*Carved crests presented by the Worshipful Company of Actuaries and former Sheriff of London and actuary Kenneth Ayers FIA in 1998.*

(© Institute of Actuaries)

Dickens might have stood his characters in the Hall and courtyard, wondering at its history and present-day beauty. That, not a smoky atmosphere, would cause them to catch their breath today.

§ 9.9 TWENTIETH-CENTURY REGENERATION AROUND STAPLE INN

The area around Staple Inn has also seen significant regeneration during the twentieth century, and especially in the later years. Recent developments have restored prosperity to the area. The huge Prudential and other office buildings are teeming with workers. Once famous Gamages at Nos. 112–128 Holborn, started in 1878 by Arthur Gamage with a five-foot frontage shop proclaiming *Tall Oaks from Small Acorns Grow* achieved great success before it was demolished in 1972, to be replaced by new buildings in 1980. The *Daily Mirror* building, the last of the great sprawling Fleet Street newspaper headquarters, was built at No. 33 Holborn in 1957–1960. Demolished in 1997 following the move of the newspapers to Docklands and elsewhere, the site is now being massively redeveloped as a great glass-fronted office building. There is huge redevelopment elsewhere in Holborn and in other areas near Staple Inn. Domestic housing is reappearing, a most welcome development. The dreadful slums have gone.

Potentially significant for Staple Inn, the former Patent Office buildings to the south of the garden, including the 'ruthlessly utilitarian section in nasty cheap cream brick'[5] have recently come into new ownership, with the prospect of major redevelopment. It would be wonderful if a more suitable design would replace the present sad mess overlooking the garden. The British Library Science Reference Information Service and the London School of Economics Library have in turn enjoyed residence here bringing the area alive with young students.

The recent great strengthening of quality in and around Staple Inn matches well its new status within the City of London. Major new developments catch the eye, but – a happy combination of old and new – all around also are images of the past.

*The City of London's best kept small garden, 1995.*

CHAPTER TEN

# *Images of the Past*

THE AREA AROUND Staple Inn is full of the ghosts of the past captured in place and street names. Some examples are given here, as a basis for further exploration.

Southampton Buildings are named after the Earl who created the Bloomsbury estate and other properties in the seventeenth century and established the form of much future West End development. Chancery Lane was originally New Street but renamed as Chancellor's Lane in 1377 when Edward III housed the Rolls of Chancery in the House for Converted Jews. Lincoln's Inn Fields evolved from two waste fields on which Lincoln's Inn students played from the fourteenth century. At the far end of the Fields, in Portsmouth Street, is the Old Curiosity Shop, built about 1567, allegedly the home of Charles Dickens's child heroine, Little Nell, and reputedly the oldest working shop in London.

To the north is Red Lion Square, where the disinterred bodies of Oliver Cromwell, Ireton and Bradshaw lay overnight before being taken to Tyburn for desecration in 1661. (Cromwell's memorial stone in Westminster Abbey reads simply, and chillingly, '1658–1661' to reflect his short stay in the Abbey.) Boswell Street is across Theobalds Road, the latter so named because it was on James I's route to his house at Theobalds in Hertfordshire. Through Gray's Inn and across Gray's Inn Road (looking south to admire Staple Inn) is Clerkenwell, originally a hamlet on well-watered meadowland (the Clerks' Well) serving a twelfth century Priory and Nunnery. Nearby Portpool Lane recalls the Portepool Fair and the Bishop of Ely's Garden. It shares its later descent into extreme slum-land with Leather Lane (probably named after a pub, the Greyhound, from the old French word leveroun), and now a popular market.

Hatton Garden, (named after Sir Christopher Hatton, Queen Elizabeth's Chancellor, and now the centre of the diamond trade), Ely Place, and the Church of St Etheldreda, (built in 1293 but with the crypt dating from 1251, with older walls possibly part of a Roman basilica), were originally part of the Bishop of Ely's domain. Ely Place was the site of his London palace from the end of the thirteenth century to 1772. Now as Crown property it is a private road with gates and a watchhouse, laid out in 1773 when local residents objected to a plan for the Fleet prison to be moved there. Greville and Brooke Streets were named after Sir Fulke Greville, first Lord Brooke, poet, who was murdered in Brooke House by a servant in 1628. Nearby Baldwin's Gardens were originally built in 1589 on the site of Brooke House by Richard Baldwin, Queen Elizabeth's gardener. Many took advantage of the privilege of sanctuary which it enjoyed, including the composer Henry Purcell who like many artists fell into debt.

In 1350 Charterhouse was a burial ground for victims of the Black Death, but soon became the foundation of a Carthusian Monastery. Also alongside Smithfield (the smoothfield and an early horse market) was St Bartholomew's Hospital, the oldest in London, founded in 1123. In the thirteenth century Saffron Hill was part of the Bishop of Ely's garden estate, growing saffron which was a key camouflage for the foul, rancid taste of so much meat. Turnmill Street echoes the numerous water mills of the area. Names such as Poultry Avenue, Cowcross Street, Lily Place, Laystall Street, Mount Pleasant, Cloth Fair, Cock Lane, Giltspur Street (originally 'Knightrider Street' from the knights who rode that way to Smithfield tournaments and where later their spurs were made), Sea Coal Lane, Stonecutter Street, Limeburner Lane, Plough Place and Bear Alley all recall earlier country scenes, trade and entertainment.

Shoe Lane is named after the old 'Sho' well at the north end of the lane. The only remaining original seventeenth-century house in Gough Square (named after a wool merchant) was Dr Johnson's home for ten years, and is open now to the public. Off Fleet Street is Clifford's Inn, and also Fetter Lane, widened in 1841, and a name with several potential origins. One is the old French *faitor*, a lawyer (although sadly seen in the thirteenth century as an idle impostor and beggar, of whom many in the lane were described in this way by Chaucer).

## CHAPTER TEN

Another possible origin is the fetters or lance vests made by armourers in the lane, and perhaps the most charitable is *frater*, for the learned brethren of the law.

Furnival Street was originally Castle Street, but renamed in the 1880s in honour of Furnival's Inn. Cursitor Street is named after the 24 Cursitors appointed to issue writs for the Court of Chancery in the sixteenth century. Aldwych is probably named after '*old wic*' – wic being the Saxon word for trading place.

And running through it all is High Holborn, separated from the bourne in the hole, or the stream in the valley, until 1869 by the Heavy Hill.

# CHAPTER ELEVEN
## *Confidence in the Future*

As the future comes 'thundering towards us' (to quote John Martin, a past President of the Institute of Actuaries), Staple Inn's history and present qualities offer much to support the view that it will play as full a part in that future as it has done in one way and another for more than eight hundred years. It is one of London's jewels, and happily recognised as such.

### § 11.1 STAPLE INN AND THE CITY

The inclusion of Staple Inn in the City in 1994 (see section 9.8) is a fitting reflection of the established and significant place of its occupants and of its architecture in today's world. The City benefits from adding this unique, longstanding and working architectural gem to its surviving treasures from the past and its many modern buildings. Staple Inn's occupants benefit from this association with the City's professions and businesses with whose work and success their own future is closely linked.

### § 11.2 STRUCTURAL AND BUSINESS CONTINUITY IN A CHANGING WORLD

Contrast the story of Lincoln's Inn's two nearby Inns of Chancery with Staple Inn. Furnival's Inn was first leased to law students in 1383. Purchased by Lincoln's Inn in 1547, it was rebuilt in 1640 to the design of Inigo Jones. Lincoln's Inn decided not to renew the lease in 1817, and the Society was dissolved. Rebuilt by another lessee in 1818–1820, the building was sold by Lincoln's Inn in 1888 and demolished by the Prudential in 1897 to allow enlargement of their headquarters.

Thavie's Inn in Shoe Lane was leased before 1422 by Lincoln's Inn, who bought the freehold in 1549. In the 1760s Lincoln's Inn declined to renew the lease, the Society was dissolved, and the Inn was sold in 1772 to help to pay for Stone Buildings at Lincoln's Inn Fields. Although John Thavie's benefaction still helps to maintain St Andrew's Church, the Inn was destroyed by fire and there is no trace of it, apart from the street and modern house of that name near Holborn Circus.

The Tudor frontage of Staple Inn, in proud if at times vulnerable splendour from the sixteenth into the twenty-first century, has been a model of continuity by comparison. With those from the eighteenth century or rebuilt after the war, Staple Inn's buildings are still good business for owner and occupants.

### § 11.3 PROFESSIONAL CONTINUITY IN A CHANGING WORLD

Gray's Inn, Barnard's Inn and Staple Inn are unique among the Inns of Court and Chancery in that this complete 'family' remains physically largely intact. They each continue actively to support educational and professional life.

Recently there have been moves to renew practical links between them. Annual visits by a Gray's Inn Reader to the 'daughter colleges' at Barnard's and Staple Inns resumed in 1997 and 1998. The lectures are on topics relevant to today's members, started again after an interval at Staple Inn of 323 years. As a separate gesture, the Institute of Actuaries decided to hold a dinner and party at Gray's Inn in 1998 to celebrate its 150th Anniversary.

Parts of Barnard's Inn, established in 1439, have vanished, but the tiny Hall remains at the end of a passage 130 metres east of Staple Inn, owned by Gresham College.

### § 11.4 LEGAL CONTINUITY OVER 900 YEARS

Another link between today and the past may be taken even further back into history, to the days when the dominant wool business carried out at *le Stapled Halle* relied on strong legal backing. Today the mathematical and other skills of actuaries need to be tempered with good appreciation of the legal circumstances relevant to their work. The same is true of other professional people working in the Inn.

The links between the occupants of Staple Inn and the legal world are now perhaps no less strong than they were in the days of the wool trade, when the pie-powder courts helped to oil the wheels of business.

### § 11.5 PAST, PRESENT AND FUTURE

Staple Inn is probably more actively occupied and enjoyed today than it ever was. The recent works to the Hall and to many offices around the courtyard have increased the attractions to tourists and visitors, and to those seeking a high quality venue for business and social occasions.

And all the while, the professional people who make this their place of work continue, as did their forebears in centuries past, to serve their public, providing whatever certainties they can to those struggling with an uncertain and sometimes hostile world.

Staple Inn provides the reassurance of a lovely place that retains its charm while adapting, sometimes dramatically, to changing, not always friendly circumstances, and comes out smiling. Can you hear and see the ghosts of the past as they encourage us into the future?

*Lithograph print of painting by William T. Chambers presented by the Society of Actuaries.*
(© Institute of Actuaries)

# References

1. Ralph Agas (1540?-1621). Staple Inn and its surroundings, 1560 – Map reduced from an original Agas map of 1560-1570 in T.Cato Worsfold (1903). *Staple Inn and its story*. London: Henry Bumpus. Original map held by Guildhall Library, Corporation of London.
2. Philip Baker and John Eversley (1999). *Multilingual capital*.
3. [Thomas Birch] (1759). *A Collection of the Yearly Bills of Mortality, from 1657 to 1758 inclusive*. London: A. Millar. Reproduced in Steven Haberman and Trevor A. Sibbett, editors (1995). *History of Actuarial Science: I. Life Tables and Survival Model*. London: William Pickering.
4. James Boswell (1740-1795). *Everybody's Boswell*. London: G Bell and Son, 1949.
5. Simon Bradley and Nikolaus Pevsner (1997). *London: I. The City of London*. Harmondsworth: Penguin Books. (The buildings of England series.)
6. G. Braun and F. Hogenberg *Atlas of London* (1572). Held by Guildhall Library, London. 1572
7. Cittie of Yorke (public house), High Holborn, London, WC1V 6RS. Leaflet issued in 2000.
8. Mr Coombe (1939). 'Staple Inn – "The Fayrest Inne of Chancerie"'. Paper read by Mr Coombe, Prudential surveyor, to the London Society on 29 July 1939. Archives of Prudential plc.
9. Archibald Day (1888). 'The History and associations of Staple Inn'. Opening Address by the President, 28 November 1887. *Journal of the Institute of Actuaries* (1888) 27 pp. 1–30
10. Charles Dickens (1836–1837). *Sketches by Boz*.
11. Charles Dickens (1838). *Oliver Twist*.
12. Charles Dickens (1841). *Barnaby Rudge*.
13. Charles Dickens (1853). *Bleak House*.
14. Charles Dickens (1861). *Great Expectations*.
15. Charles Dickens (1870). *The Mystery of Edwin Drood*.
16. *Dictionary of National Biography*. Oxford: University Press.
17. P J Edwards (1898). *History of London Street Improvements, 1855–1897*. P. S. King and Sons, for London County Council, 1898.
18. John Evelyn (1620–1706). *The diary of John Evelyn* edited by E.S. de Beer, Oxford University Press, 1959. Cited in Malcom Billings, *London: a companion to its history and archaeology*. London: Kyle Cathie.
19. Douglas Morey Ford (1908). *Written in red – a secret of Staple Inn*. London: Hurst and Blackett.
20. Robert Goddard (1989). *Painting the Darkness*. London: Bantam Press.
21. John Gower (ca.1330-1408). Cited in Eileen Power (1937). *Medieval People*. Harmondsworth: Penguin Books.
22. Frank E. Guaschi (1994). 'The Old Staple Inn'. *The Actuary*, September p. 30
23. Nathaniel Hawthorne (1855). *Passages from the English Notebooks*.
24. W Herbert (1804). *Antiquities of the Inns of Court and Chancery; containing historical and descriptive sketches relative to their original foundation, customs, ceremonies, buildings, government, etc, etc, with a concise history of the English Law*. London: Vernor and Hood, J. Storer and J. Greig.
25. Cecil A. Hewitt (1980). 'Examples of the Renaissance and after (1581–1890): Staple Inn, High Holborn, London.' *English historic carpentry*. Phillimore, 1980
26. Roger Hudson (1998). *London: Portrait of a City*. Folio Society, London, 1998.
27. Institute of Actuaries (1948). 'The Old Hall of Staple Inn'. *Journal of the Institute of Actuaries* 72 (1948).
28. Institute of Actuaries (1998). *Tapestry in Staple Inn Hall*. March 1998
29. Stephen Inwood (1998). *A history of London*. Macmillan, London, 1998
30. E. F. Jacob (1961). *Oxford history of England: the fifteenth century 1399–1485*. London
31. Philip M. Johnston (1918). 'Architectural notes on Staple Inn'. Paper read to London and Middlesex Archaeological Society at Staple Inn meeting on 23 March 1918
32. Sir Frank Morgan (1955). Staple Inn restored. At reopening by Sir Hartley Shawcross, Treasurer of Gray's Inn.
33. Maurice E. Ogborn (1964). *Staple Inn*. London: Institute of Actuaries.
34. Samuel Pepys (1633–1703). Everybody's Pepys Diary: *The Diary of Samuel Pepys, 1660-1669*. London: G Bell and Son.

# REFERENCES

35. *A Perfect Diurnal of the passages of Parliament.* May 1643.

36. Lisa Pickard (2000). *Dr Johnson's London: life in London 1740–1770.* Weidenfeld and Nicolson, 2000.

37. W. E. Pocock (1838). *Report on Metropolis Improvements.*

38. Board of Prudential Insurance Company. Minute Books. Entries for Staple Inn in minutes of 25 November, 2, 9, 16 December, 1886; 11 June, 16 September, 10 December 1936; 11 March, 10 June, 23 September, 20 December 1937; 4 August and 10 November 1938. Archives of Prudential plc.

39. Prudential Insurance Company (1905). Letter to *The Times*, August 1905. Archives of Prudential plc.

40. *The Prudential Bulletin*, October 1924, p. 689, 'Holborn's Oasis'.

41. *The Prudential Bulletin*, May 1936.

42. Registrar-General of Births, Deaths and Marriages in England and Wales (1843). *Fifth annual report of births, deaths and marriages in England.* English Life Table No. 1.

43. John Richardson (2000). *The annals of London: a year-by-year record of a thousand years of history.* London: Cassell, 2000.

44. R.C. Simmonds (1948). *The Institute of Actuaries 1848–1948: an account of the Institute of Actuaries during its first hundred years.* Cambridge: University Press.

45. Sketch map of Staple Inn area in 1520. Map held by Corporation of London Guildhall Library.

46. John Stow (1525-1605?). *A Survey of London.* 1598.

47. John Stow (1525–1605?). *The Chronicles of England.* 1580. Later posthumously *Annales, Or, A Generall Chronicle of England.* 1631.

48. *The Times*, late August 1886.

49. *The Times*, 3 November 1886.

50. *The Times*, 19 November 1886.

51. *The Times*, 27 November 1886.

52. G. M. Trevelyan (1928). *History of England.* London: Longman, Green and Co.

53. Anthony Trollope (1864). *Can you forgive her?* Chapter 61.

54. Ben Weinreb and Christopher Hibbert, editors. (1987). *The London Encyclopaedia*, (1987). London: Macmillan.

55. E. Williams (1906). *Staple Inn customs house, wool court and Inn of Chancery: its medieval surroundings and associations.* London: Archibald Constable.

56. Gwynn A. Williams (1963). *Medieval London from commune to capital.* London: Athlone.

57. Graham Wingham. Recollection in October 2000 by Mr Graham Wingham of Sanford Bros., the jewellers at No. 3 Holborn, of remarks passed down through the family by his grandfather's brother who was on fire duty at Staple Inn when the bomb exploded.

58. T.Cato Worsfold (1903). *Staple Inn and its story.* London: Henry Bumpus.

### SOME OTHER SOURCES USED

John Baker (2001). *Readers and readings in the Inns of Court and Chancery.* (Selden Society Supplementary Series 13). London: Selden Society.

Arthur Bryant (1953). *The story of England: makers of the realm.* London: Collins.

David Crystal, editor (1998). *The Cambridge Biographical Encyclopaedia.* Second edition. Cambridge University Press, 1998.

Laurie Dennett (1998). *A sense of security: 150 years of Prudential.* Cambridge: Granta Editions, 1998.

Juliet Gardiner and Neil Wenborn, editors (1995). *The History Today Companion to British History.* London: Collins and Brown, 1995.

Juliet Gardiner, editor (2000). *Who's Who in British History.* London: Collins and Brown.

Maurice E Ogborn. [1964]. [Manuscript 'Historical Notes on Staple Inn' prepared in relation to his booklet *Staple Inn*. London: Institute of Actuaries, 1964.]

*The Oxford English Reference Dictionary.* 2nd ed., Oxford University Press, 1996.

Angela Partington, editor (1996). *The Oxford Dictionary of Quotations.* Fourth revised edition. University Press.

Roy Porter (1996). *London: a social history.* Harmondsworth: Penguin Books.

Edward Rutherfurd (1998). *London: the novel.* London: Arrow Books.

Charles Sparrow (1998). 'The fayrest Inne'. *British Actuarial Journal* 4 p.1059-1069. The 'Gray's Inn Reading' 1998.

Paul Thornton (1998). A Historical Perspective on the Actuarial Profession and Thought in the UK. *Transactions of the 26th International Congress of Actuaries* volume 2.

# Index

References to illustrations show the page numbers in **bold**

## A
'a ring, a ring'  53
Actuarial Tuition Service  75
Adelphi Terrace  70
affluence and squalor contrast  23
Albert Embankment  59
alcohol  54
Aldermanbury  77
Aldwych  86
ale houses  54
Alfred the Great, King  8, 18
ambidexter  49
American Academy of Actuaries  81, **82**
Anglo-Saxon tribal custom  18
Anne, Queen  49
Antwerp  14
Ascension Day  23
attorneys  49
Ayers, Kenneth  81, **83**

## B
'Baa baa black sheep'  13–14
Bacon, Sir Francis  26, 29, 80
Bagehot, Charles  28
Baker, John  50
Baldwin's Gardens  85
Baldwin, Richard  85
Barbon, Nicholas  44
Barnard's Inn  20, 22, 29, 31, 47, 55, 66, 87
barrister (word)  19
barrister qualification by general consent  31
barristers  49, 79
Bartholomew Fair  56
Bayswater Road  23
Bear Alley  85
bear-baiting  34
beards' legislation  21
beating the bounds  23
'beau-traps'  35
Beaumont, John  12
Beckton sewers  59
Bede, Venerable  39
Bedford, Duke of  53
Bedlam  34
beggars  34
Benchers  19
best-kept small garden award  79, **83**
Bethlehem Royal Hospital  34
betting  34
Bills of Mortality  39, **40**
Bishop of Ely's Garden  85
Bishopsgate  10
Black Death  15, 85
Black Friars monastery  19
Black Swan [gin distillery]  55
Black Swan [inn]  34
Blackfriars Theatre  32
Boadicea, Queen  7
bolts  21, 33
Boston  13
Boswell Street  56, 85
Boswell, James  34, 51, 56
Brabent  14
Bradley, Simon  27, 78
Bradshaw, George  85
brandy-shops  54
Braun, G  22
brick making  43
British Library  84
British Museum  56
Broad Street  43
Brocket, Nicholas  27–28, 50
Brooke House  85
Brooke Street  85
Brooke, Lord  85
Brumfit [shop]  70, 75
Brumfit, John  70
Buck, Sir George  24, 30
*Builder, The*  67
building regulations after Great Fire  43
building signs  35, 53
'bull in a china shop'  34
Bunhill Fields  58
Bunny, Edmund  21
bus services  64

## C
cabriolet  64
Caesars busts  47, 48, 67
Calais  15
Calan, Antonio [Canaletto]  **33**
Callis, Robert  31
Cambridge University  18
Camden Borough  79
Camden, Lord  49
Canadian Institute of Actuaries  81, **82**
Canning, George  33
Canute, King  8–9
Carlyle, Thomas  64
carp  72
Cary, Thomas  30
Casanova  55
case-study approach, early form  21
Castle Street  86
Catherine of Aragon, Queen  23
Caxton, William  19
Cecil, Lord  21
Central Line  64
*certum ex incertis*  5, 79
cesspits  58, 59
chamber pots  35
Chambré, Sir Alan  48, **48**
Champion, Richard  26, **26**, 27, 28, 30, 49
Chancellor's Lane  85
Chancery  11
Chancery Court  17
Chancery Lane  11, 12, 14, 15, 18, 19, 35, 55, 85
Chancery Lane underground station  76
Charles I, King  28, 29, 38, 39, 47, 49
Chartered Insurance Institute  77
Charterhouse  85
Chatham Place  70
Chaucer, Geoffrey  19, 85
Cheapside  43
Chelsea  35
Chelsea Embankment  59
Chester, Chief Justice of  19
Chichester, Bishop of  12, 13
cholera  58, 59
Church power  18
Cittie of York (public house)  22
City of London
  legal training not allowed within  18
  temporarily united with Westminster  38
  Volunteer Corps  72
civil disorder  16
Civil War  31, 38–39, **39**, 44
claret, dozen bottles  48
Clarkson [shop]  75
Clement's Inn  66
clergy as advocates  18
Clerk's Well, The  85
Clerkenwell  56, 58, 85
Clerkenwell Road  56
Clerkenwell workhouse  58
Clifford's Inn  85
climate  33
Clink Liberty  32
clock in the Hall  45, 47
clock weights  73–74
Cloth Fair  85
cloth trade  15
cloth-making industry  15
Coal, Corn and Finance Committee  67
coats of arms  24
Cock Lane  85
cock-fights and cockpits  34
coffee houses and taverns  34, 58
Colchester  7
*Comedy of Errors, The*  32
Commissioners of Works and Buildings  67
Common Council  38
common law  17, 18
Commons Preservation Society  67
Company of the Merchants of the Staple  24
Congreve, William  24
conventicles  51
Converts, House of  13
Coombe, Mr  74
Coram's Fields  53
Coram, Thomas  53, 79

# INDEX

Cordwainers Company 58
Cornhill 7, 34
Corporation of London 80
Cotswolds 10
Court of Chancery 86
Court of Common Council 67
Court of Common Pleas 48, 75
courts of justice 17
Covent Garden 35, 39
Cowcross Street 85
Cowper, Lord Chancellor 49
Cox, Lord Chief Justice 55
Crawley, Sir Francis 31, 75
cress 56
crime 34, 53
Cromwell, Oliver 38, 39, 44, 85
Crowther, J 67
Cuckfield Park 26
cupboard (word) 27
Cursitor Street 86
Cursitors 86
Curtain Theatre 32
customs duties 13, 14

## D

*Daily Mirror* building 84
Day, Archibald 47
dead carts 40
Derby, Robert Earl of 11
Dickens, Charles
  *Barnaby Rudge* 55
  Barnard's Inn 47
  *Bleak House* 59, 62
  Furnival's Inn 62
  if writing today 83
  Middle Row 23, 63
  *Mystery of Edwin Drood, The* 23, 30, 45, 62–63
  *Oliver Twist* 58
  *Pickwick Papers, The* 62
  *Sketches by Boz* 64
  Staple Inn connections and references 62–63

*Dictionary of National Biography* 50
disease 53, 58
Dispensary for relief of the infant poor 53
'distance learning' 44
*Diurnal, The* 38
Domesday survey 9
Dordrecht 14
dragons, silver 10
drainage system 59
Drury Lane 8, 39
Dryden, John 32
Duke of York's Theatre 39

## E

earthquake 1580 26
Edgware Road 23
Edison, Thomas Alva 71
Edward I, King 11, 12, 13, 14, 18
Edward II, King 11, 14
Edward III, King 15, 16, 18, 85
Edward the Confessor, King 9
electric lifts 64
electric lighting 71
Elizabeth I, Queen 28, 34, 48, 85
Ely Fair 10
Ely House 34
Ely Palace 11
Ely Place 10, 16, 23, 85
Ely, Bishops of 10, 11, 34, 85
Engham, Vincent 27, 30
English Heritage 80
English language 16, 18
Euston Road 53
Euston station 64
Evelyn, John 41
Exchequer 11
executions, public 23–24, **25**
'Experience foretells' 81
extra-parochial status 35

## F

Faculty of Actuaries 78, 81, **82**, 83
fairs and markets 10
Family Endowment Society 70
Farringdon Market 56
Farringdon Road 56
Farringdon Street 51, 56
'Fayrest Inne of Chancery, The' 30
Ferres, Earl of 24, **25**
Festing, H 67
Fetter Lane 23, 26, 30, 32, 34, 41, 44, 51, 85–86
Field Lane 58
Fielding, Henry 53
fig tree 49
Finlaison, John 78
fire watching 76
First World War 72
Fishman, Alan 81, **81**
Fleet Market 56
Fleet prison 15, 16, 23, 54, 55, 85
Fleet river 14, 15, 19, 23, 44, 51
Fleet Street 12, 14, 16, 18, 22, 30, 41, 43, 54, 84, 85
Flemish weavers 15
flying bombs 76, 77
Fortescue, John 20
forts around London 38, **39**
Foundling Hospital 53, 79
French language 18
frost fair 33, **33**
Furnival Street 12, 86
Furnival's Inn 22, 67, 79, 86, 87

## G

Gable, Joanne 75
gallows 23
Gamages [shop] 84
games and sports 34
'Gaol of London' 23
Gay, John 24
General Post Office 71
General Strike 1926
Genoese merchants 15

*Gentleman's Magazine* 34, 45, 53
Gerard, John 32
Giltspur Street 85
gin 54
Gin Act 1751 54
*Gin Lane* **54**
Globe Theatre 32
Goddard & Gibbs 79
Godwin, George 58
Golden Anchor [inn] 50
Googe, Barnabe 21
Gordon riots 55
Gordon, Lord 55
Gough Square 50, 85
Gower, John 17
Grand Company and Fellows of Staple Inn 20
Grand moots 21
grassy hill, a 7, 19
Graunt, John **40**
Gray's Inn 18, 19, 31, 47, 48, 77, 85, 87
  Ancients 65
  Barnard's Inn as daughter body 20
  Benchers of 20
  cockpit nearby 34
  Coffee House 58
  effective separation from Staple Inn 47
  Hall 32
  independence of Staple Inn 26, 30
  Readers 20
  Staple Inn as daughter body 20
Gray's Inn Road 22, 23, 39, 58, 85
Gray, Sir Reginald 19
Great Fire 1666: 41–44, **42**, **43**
Great Plague 1665: 39–40, **40**
Great stink 1858: 59
Gresham College 20, 87
Gretna Green 54, 55
Greville Street 85
Greville, Sir Fulke 85
Greyhound [public house] 85

Guaschi, Frank 77
Guildhall 8
Guilford Street 39
Gunpowder Alley 41
gunpowder plot 29
gunpowder stores 41

## H

hackney carriages 33, 64
**Hall, The**
  1580 notable features 26
  1580–1581 building 26
  1580s design 26
  1655 roof rebuilt 39
  1882 views **46**, **67**
  1996–97 refurbishment 80
  adornments removed by Ancients 47
  central heating 71
  clock 45, 47
  contents removed by Ancients 67
  cornice lamps 73
  demolished by flying bomb 76–77
  electric lighting 71
  floor rushes 27
  flying bomb damage **76**
  gallery 26
  gas lighting 71
  hammer-beam roof 26–27
  heating 27
  hirings 83
  lighting 80
  paintings 48, 49
  roof beams 72
  roof fall after flying bomb explosion 76–77
  roof trusses 80
  sculpture 48
  seating 71
  seating arrangements 71–72
  stained glass 12, 22, 26, 27–30, **28**, **29**, 47, **47**, 48, **48**, 75, 79–80, **80**, 81, **82**
  stalagmites on beams 27

# INDEX

**Hall, The** continued
steel frame to roof 72
tapestry 81, **81**
tie-rods inserted in beams 70
wainscot 27
wall panels 47
weddings 83
Hampstead 58
Handel, George Frederick 53
hangings, public 24, 53
Hanseatic merchants 13
Hardy, Sir George Francis 78
Harris (author) 55
Harvard Business School 21
Hatton Garden 33, 53, 58, 85
Hatton, Sir Christopher 34, 85
Hawthorne, Nathaniel title page, 60
'Heavy Hill' **14**, 15, 86
Henry II, King 17, 18
Henry III, King 11, 17, 18
Henry V, King 14
Henry VIII, King 14, 23
Herbert, W 49
Hewitt, C A 77
Heywood, Thomas 32
High Holborn 7, 86
highwaymen 34
Hobbes, Thomas 26
Hogarth, William 10, 34, 54, **54**
Hogenberg, F 22
Holborn 9, 10, 11, 32, 34, 40, 50, 56, 58, 64, 84
  first suburb of London 7
Holborn Bars 10, 19, 22
Holborn Bridge 14, 15, 19, 41, 44, 51
Holborn Conduit 60
Holborn District Board 62
Holborn Hill 24
Holborn road 12, 14, 15, 16, 22, 23, 30, 43, 44, 53, 62
Holborn Viaduct 62, 64, **64**, 71
Holborn Viaduct station 64
Holborn, High Constable of 53

Holebourne 34
Holywell Priory 32
home staple policy abandoned 15
'Honour in sincerity and tolerance' 81
horse-dung 35
Hospital for women 58
House for Converted Jews 85
house numbering 53
House of Converts 12
Hull 13
hung prisoners' heads impaled 24
hustings 17
Hutton, Sir Richard 28–29, 38

### I
'I hold every man a debtor to his profession' 80, **80**
*Illustrated London News* 62
'I'm just a little girl lost in the fog' 59
incendiary bombs 76
influenza 58
Inn (word) 19
Inner Temple 19, 24, 41, 48, 76
Inns of Apprentices 18
Inns of Chancery 18, 19, 31, 35, 49, 66
  daughter bodies of Inns of Court 19
  Staple Inn the first 20
Inns of Court 18, 19, 20, 31, 35, 49, 66
**Institute of Actuaries**
1887 Annual General Meeting 69
1887 celebratory dinner 69
1941 examinations 75
1948 centenary celebrations 77
1955 return to Staple Inn 79
1973 125th anniversary 79
1998 150th anniversary 81
busts of actuaries 78
coat of arms 79, **79**
Council Chamber 78, 79

Council table and chairs 73, 77
dinners 83
Elderton room 79
General Purposes Committee 69
Library 71, 72, 77–78
Lidstone room 79
long term use of Staple Inn 83
mace 78
meetings post-flying bomb 77
membership 83
motto 79
Phelps room 79
President's Room 79
previous accommodation 70
Redington room 79
rents Staple Inn 69
Royal Charter 79
Staple Inn Buildings 72
Statistical Society 70
war memorials 78
women members 72
Institute of Actuaries' Students Society 72, 78, 79, **80**
insurance against fire 44
interregnum 39
Inwood, Stephen 59
Ireton, Henry 85
Irish famine 56
Irish immigrants 56
Isle of Thanet 8
Italian merchants 13, 15

### J
James I, King 23, 28, 31, 85
Jefferson, J C 54
Jenkyn, Robert 45, 47, 48
Jews 11–12
John of Gaunt 16
John, King 9
Johnson, Samuel 38, 50–51, 54, 55, 56, 85
Johnston, Philip 26
Jones, Inigo 87

Jonson, Ben 32
Judge of the Common Pleas 29, 30
Justice of the Common Pleas 48
justice system 18

### K
Kelham, Robert 50
Kendall, Timothy 21
Kilburne, Richard 44, 50
Kilburne, Robert 50
King's Bench 26, 48, 50
King's College 70
King's Cross 51
King's Cross station 64
King's Justices 19
King's Theatre 39
Knight, Reginald 30, 47
Knightrider Street 85
Knights Hospitallers 19
Knights Templar 13, 19
Knightsbridge 35

### L
Lancaster, Duchy of 11
Land Registry Office 67
Langdale [distiller] 55
Law Courts 18
law merchants 17
law schools 18
Law Society 49, 77
law students 18
lawyers 17–19
Laystall Street 85
laystalls 23, 58
le Brun, Mary 11
Leadenhall 11
Leather Lane 85
Leech, Thomas 26, 45, **45**
legal charges 45, 47
legal education 19, 39, 49
legal process 17
legal profession
  effective 'closed shop' 31

privileged classes 31
role in English country families 32
leper hospital 22
leprosy 39
Liberties of the Fleet 54
Lidstone, George James 77
life expectation 53, 58
Lily Place 85
Limeburner Lane 85
Lincoln's Inn 18, 19, 20, 29, 31, 87
Lincoln's Inn Chapel 72
Lincoln's Inn Fields 39, 85, 87
Lincoln's Inn Fields Theatre 32
Lincoln, Bishop of 13
Lincoln, Earl of 19
Liquorpond Street 56
Little Parliament 44
live animals driven through streets 53, 58
Lombard Street 71
**London**
Anglo-Saxons 8
charter 9
children's languages 12th century 10
City and Westminster 9
commune 9
constitution 9
Danes 8
Fire 115 AD 7
first inhabitants 7
first suburb 7
fogs 35, 59, **59**, 64
Great Fire 1666 41–44, **42**, **43**
illicit housing 35
international character and trade 10
Lord Mayor 9, 80
*Lundenwic* 8
Parliament support in Civil War 38, **39**
Romans 7

# INDEX

**London** continued
  sanitation 19th century 58–61
  Saxons 8
  sewerage system 59
  three hills 7
  tolls 8
  trade growth 9th & 10th
    centuries 8
  walking tours 83
  wall 8
London Bridge 24, 32–33, 41
London Central Meat Market 58
*London Chronicle* 49
London defensive bulwark 38
London Metropolitan Water
  Company 31
London Open House weekends
  83
London Public Dispensary 58
London School of Economics
  Library 84
London Society 74
London's population
  100 AD 7
  8th century 8
  1348–1350: 15
  1380: 15
  1500–1600: 26
  1600–1700: 35, 38
  18th century 53
  19th century 56
  population explosion 58
  religious orders 18
London's UndergrounD 64
'looking glasses' 35
Lord Chancellor's Department
  18, 19
lottery draws 34
Lovell, Paul 41
Ludgate Hill 7, 41
lunatics 34
Lundenwic 8
Lynn 13
Lyon, Stewart 83

## M

Macclesfield, Earl of 49
Magna Carta 9
Malcolm, John 54
Malines 14
Malmesbury, Monastery of 12
Mansell, Robert 28, 30
Mansfield, Lord 48
Marble Arch 23
market gardens 35
markets and fairs 10
Marlowe, Christopher 32
marriages, quick and cheap 54
marrying houses 54
Marsden, William 58
Martin Ashley Architects 80
Martin, John 87
Marylebone Road 53
Maufe, Sir Edward 77
Mayors of the Staple 11
McAlpine and Sons, Sir Robert 77
McLean [highwayman] 24
Medici, Marie de **43**
medicinal wells and spas 51
Merchant Adventurers 15
Merchants of the Staple 15
Middle Row **22**, 22–23, 31, 35, 50,
  53, 60–62, **61**, 63, 64
Middle Temple 19, 47, 48, 76, 77
monasteries 32
Moncur, Jennie 81, **81**
Moorfields 34, 41, 43
moots 21, 33
Moreton Hall 73
Morgan, Sir Frank 78–79
*Morning Post, The* 72
Mount Pleasant 39, 85
murders 16
Murdoch, John 50
Museum of London 80

## N

Napier, John 78
New Covent Garden Theatre 32
New Model Army 39
New Oxford Street 22, 64
New Street 85
Newgate 8, 14, 41
Newgate prison 15, 16, 23, 24, 55
night cart men 58–59
nosegays 23, 24
nursery rhyme 13–14

## O

Oates, Titus 24
obelisks, granite 10
Old Bailey 41, 71
Old Bourne 30
old buildings, public views on
  preservation 69
Old clothes Men 73, **73**
Old Curiosity Shop 85
*Olde Tobacco Shoppe, Ye* 70
Ordnance Survey 59
organised gangs 53
Oxford Street 64
Oxford University 18

## P

Paine, Tom 51
Pall Mall 39
*Pall Mall Gazette* 47
parchment discoveries 75
Parker, Archbishop 21
parliamentarians 38
parliaments 17
Patent Office 78
Patent Office buildings 84
Pauls Chain 41
Peacham, Henry 35
Pearson, James 48
Peasants' Revolt 1381 16
Pentonville Road 53
Pepys, Samuel 34, 40, 41
Pevsner, Nikolaus 27, 78
pewter plates 51
Phelps, W P 73
Phylpe, William 75
pie-powder courts 16, 17, 88
plague
  664 AD 39
  1563, 1574, 1581: 26
  1593, 1625: 39
  1665 Great Plague 39–30, **40**
  elimination 44
  recurring 15
Plough Place 85
poll tax 16
poors hole 58
Pope, Thomas 27–28
Portepool Fair 10, 85
Portpool Lane 85
Portsmouth Street 85
Poultry Avenue 85
poverty, extreme 34
Poxwell 15
'Praise God Barebones' 44
Presbyterian treatise 75
Pretorian Way 8
printing 44
prisoners, condemned 15, 24
prize-fighting 34
property acquisition by marriage 19
prosperity in Elizabethan England
  26
Prudential Assurance Company 67,
  69, 74, 77, 78–79, 80, 84, 87
  long term care of Staple Inn 83
  office building in Holborn Bars
    10, **74**
  rents Staple Inn to the Institute of
    Actuaries 69
  water under office building 30–31
*Prudential Bulletin* 32
public executions 15, 24, **25,** 53
public holidays for hangings 24
Public Record Office 13
public transport, 19th century 64
public whippings 23–24, 53
Pudding Lane 41
Purcell, Henry 85
Purpoole in Holborn, Ancient
  Manor of 19
*Puteus oppletus* 72

## Q

Queen's Head [inn] 50

## R

Raleigh, Sir Walter 29
readings 21
red cross mark to denote plague 40
Red Lion Square 33, 44, 53, 55, 56,
  58, 85
Reed, Isaac 50
religious dissenters 51
restoration of the monarchy 39
retailing, development of 22
Reynolds, Sir Joshua 51
Richard I, King 9, 11, 18
Richardson, Samuel 50
ring road 53
riots
  anti-Irish 55
  food 34
  Gordon riots 1780: 55
  Irish march 1848: 56
  no popery 55
  Shoe Lane 55
  stench 23
road maintenance 14–15, 30, 35, 38,
  63
road transport 33–34
robbers 34
Robinson, John 50
Rochester 62
Rolls Chapel 12
Rolls of Chancery 13, 85
Roman amphitheatre 8
Roman law 18
Roman roads 7, 14
Rose Theatre 32
Round Church 19
Royal Academy 56
Royal Chancery 19
Royal Commission on Inns of

# INDEX

Court and Chancery 66
Royal Fine Arts Committee 74
Royal Free Hospital 58
Royal justice system 17
Rude Children playing 73, **73**
'Ruffians Hall' 34
Rules of the Fleet 54
Rymer, Thomas 14

## S
saffron 85
Saffron Hill 53, 58, 85
St Andrew's Church 8, **14**, 15, 19, 23, 26, 39, 40, 41, 44, **52**, 56, 58, **64** 76, 79, 87
St Andrew's parish 55
St Bartholomew's Hospital 23, 40, 85
St Ethelreda's Church 11, 85
St Giles 35, 40, 43, 44, 53, 54, 58, 64
St Giles in the Fields 60
St James's 39
St James's Square 70
St Michael's Alley 34
St Omer 14
St Paul's 12
St Paul's Cathedral 41
St Paul's church 14
St Sepulchres church 24
St-Giles-in-the-Fields 22, 24
Sanford Brothers [shop] 79
Savoy Palace 16
Scrope's Inn 19
Sea Coal Lane 85
Sedan chairs 34
Sedgly, Jonas 48
Select Committee on Metropolis Improvements 62
Serjeant's Inn 18, 19, 66, 69
Serjeant-at-Law 48, 66
sewerage system 58, 59
Sewers, Commissioner of 31
Shakespeare, William 10, 16, 32, 50

Shepherd, Jack 24
Sherborne, Battle of 38
Sherringtons [shop] 79
ship money 29
Shoe Lane 12, 19, 34, 41, 55, 85, 87
shoe patten 75, **75**
Shoreditch 32
Silchester 7
six shillings and eight pence 45, 47
Sloane, Sir Hans 51
Smithfield 16, 23, 53, 56, 58, 85
Smithfield Market 34, **57**, 58
Smythe, Francis C Domville 47
social decline 51
Society for the Preservation of Ancient Buildings 74
Society for the Protection of Ancient Buildings 67
Society of Actuaries 81, **82**
**Society of Staple Inn** 20–24
  buildings 21–22
  decline 44
  dinners 27, 49, **51**, 66
  disclaim involvement with legal profession 66
  entry fees 49
  fees for guests 49
  fines 49
  freehold of Staple Inn acquired 65
  good maintenance of property 49
  Gray's Inn Reader 21
  Gray's Inn, independence from 26
  legal instruction 21
  mace 24, 27, 65, 78, **78**
  membership 66
  notable students 21
  port wine 49
  Principal, Ancients and Grandfellows 20
  Principals 23, 44, 49–50
  Principals' stained glass windows 47

  trustees 65–66
  twelve bottles of good clarett 49
  winding up of the Society 65–66
  woolsack insignia 24
Society of the Merchants of Staple, The 11
Society of the Protection of Ancient Buildings 70
Soho Fields 39
Soho Square 58
solicitors 49
Southampton 13, 15
Southampton Buildings 13, 76, 85
Southampton Row 53, 67
Southampton, Earl of 13, 85
Southwark 13, 85
Spencer, John 79, **79**
Spiers, Dorothy 72
'splitting hairs' 21
sports with animals 34
Sprague, Thomas Bond 78
stagecoaches 34, 63–64
stained glass 12, 22, 26, 27–30, **28**, **29**, 47, **47**, 48, **48**, 75, 79–80, **80**, 81, **82**
Stanley, William 67
staple (word) 10–11
Staple Halls 10
**Staple Inn**
  1313 surroundings sketch map **13**
  1560 surroundings sketch map **21**
  1580–92 rebuilding 26–27
  16th and 17th centuries 32–34
  1666 Great Fire 41, **43**
  18th and 19th centuries residents 50
  1756 fire 45
  18th century rebuilding 45
  1801–1884 'a little nook' 56, 83
  1855 an American view 60
  1886 plan **70**
  1887 restoration 70
  1890s earliest photograph **71**
  1903 courtyard **73**

  1926 General Strike 73
  1936 survey 74
  1937–39 restoration 74
  1944 flying bomb 45, **76**
  1954–1955 rebuilding 77–79
  1955 re–opening ceremony 78
  1993–1998 refurbishment 79–82
  Ancients' independence 20
  archives lost 45
  Ascension Day 23
  beating the bounds 23
  bought by G Trollope and Sons 67
  building services 80
  car parking 73
  cesspools 31
  City of London – now part of 87
  City of London Volunteer Corps 72
  clocks 78
  contemporary activity 88
  Council chamber 78, **78**
  daughter body of Gray's Inn 20
  early improvements made by Institute of Actuaries 71
  effective separation from Gray's Inn 47
  Elizabethan black and white half-timbered buildings 22, 27, 43, **43**, 60, 70
  ex-parochial status 23
  'The Fayrest Inne of Chancery' 30
  first buildings 12
  First World War 72
  fountain 78
  freehold bought by Society of Staple Inn 65
  garden 32
  gates 24
  ghosts of the past 88
  Gray's Inn, independence from 30
  Holborn front, steel frame 77
  Holborn road frontage 22
  images of the past 84

  included in City boundaries 79
  inhabitants 31
  initials PJT 45, 62
  initials TLP 45
  initials TPW 45
  Inn of Chancery 16
  insignia on stained glass window 48
  intellectual life 32
  land tax assessment 50
  libraries 50
  listing grades I and II 80–81
  little nook 56, 83
  local public transport 64
  postal boundary 67
  'practically a Club' 49
  Principal removed 30
  Principals, election 30
  privileged classes 31
  public opinion before auction 67
  Reader 20
  reconstruction largely as before 77
  Romans 7
  roof trusses 77
  social life 32
  sold by auction 68–69
  South door **45**
  spartan living conditions 38
  springs 31
  stench 23
  structure without restoration for 350 years 74
  student numbers 31
  tapestry 81
  temporarily united with City of London 39
  timber frontage 43
  trading centre established 12
  Tudor bow windows 70
  Tudor frontage 87
  unruly disturbances 30
  water supply 31, 71
  well 72, **73**

## INDEX

Staple Inn Buildings 72
Staple Inn Chambers 79
Staple Inn Publishing Company 73
Staple Inn Society 20, 21
Staple towns 11
**Stapled Halle, le** 10–16
  13th century 12
  13th–14th century trade growth 13
  14th century neighbours 12
  access to River Thames 14
  customs-house operation 17
  meaning of words 10–11
  nearness to Chancery Lane 20
  pie-powder court 17
  Society of Staple Inn 20
  tenements leased 12
  trade decline 15
  trading ends 16
  wool trade 10–16
  wool trade and legal backing 87–88
Staples (towns) 10, 14
Staples, Sir John 67
Star Chamber 34
Starcolf, Richard 12
Steevens, George 50
stench of River Fleet 19
Stephen, King 9
Stone Buildings 87
Stonecutter Street 85
Stow, John 12
Strand 18, 32
street fights 53
street noise 35
street-gulleys 59
sung grace 83
Swift, Jonathan 24, 35

### T

'taking the wall' 38
'Tall Oaks from Small Acorns Grow' 84
Talleyrand-Périgord, Charles 50
tax centre towns 11
taxation 11
Taxing Masters in Chancery 65, **65**, 67
telephone 71
television 78, 79
Temple 18, 19
Temple Bar 24
Temple Church 16, 41
Thames Water tours 59
Thames, River 32–33, **33**, 59
Thavie's Inn 22, 31, 87
Thavie, John 87
Thavies Inn [street name] 87
theatres 32, 39
Theobalds Road 85
'Third University of England' 18, 72
Thompson, John 45
*Times, The* 50, 66, 67
Tokenhouse Yard 69
Tot-hill 39
Tower of London 10, 41
'Town and Gown' 34
town swamps 58
Trafalgar Square 8
traffic congestion 53, 60, 64
Trained Bands 38
tram services 64
Trayle, Thomas 28
trolley-bus poles 75
Trollope and Sons, G 67, 68
Trollope, Anthony 60
tuberculosis 58
Turk's Head bagnio 55
Turnmill Street 85
'Twopenny Tube' 64
Tyburn gallows 15, 23, 24, 53, 85
Tyler, Wat 16
typewriters 71
typhus 58

### U

Underground 76
Unincreasable Club 50
United State Consul, Liverpool 60

### V

vagabonds 34, 53
Victoria Embankment 59
Victoria station 64
Victoria, Queen 58
Voltaire, François 51

### W

walkway etiquette **36–37**, 38
Walmesley, Sir Thomas 28, 29, 31
Walmisley, Edward 47
War Damage Commission 77
Warburton, Sir Peter 29, 31
Ward, Ned 56
Ward, Samuel 50
Warde, Thomas 45, 47, **47**, 48
Warner, Dr 55
Warner, Robert 20
wartime shelters 76
Warwick Lane 41
water pipes 35
watercress girls 56, 58
Waterhouse, Alfred 69, 70
Waterloo station 64
Watling Street 23, 41
Welch, Mr 53
Wesley, John 51
Westminster
  and City of London 9, 38
  coronation 1066 9
  fair 11
  Great Hall 17
  parliaments 17
  Staple 11
Westminster Abbey 85
Weymouth 15
White Friars 19, 53
White Horse [inn] 34
Whitehall and Holborn Improvement Act 1865 62
wigmakers 22
Wilkes, John 48
Willett, Robert 27
William the Conqueror, King 9
Williams, E 22, 49
Winchester, Bishop of 32
Wood, Hutton **78**
wool merchants 20, 50
wool trade 10–16, 17, 88
woollen cloth trade 15
Woolmen's Company 24
Woolsack 17
Woolsack insignia 24, **78**
Wordsworth, Richard 50, 56
Wordsworth, William 50, 56
workman killed 1919 72
World War I 72, 78
World War II 75–77
  flying bomb 1944 45, **76**
  war memorial 78
Worsfold, T C 16, 72
Worshipful Company of Actuaries 81, 83, **83**
Wren, Sir Christopher 44
Wycliffe, John 19

### Y

Yates, Sir Joseph 48, **48**
York 34
York Minster 21

### Z

Zeppelin raid 72